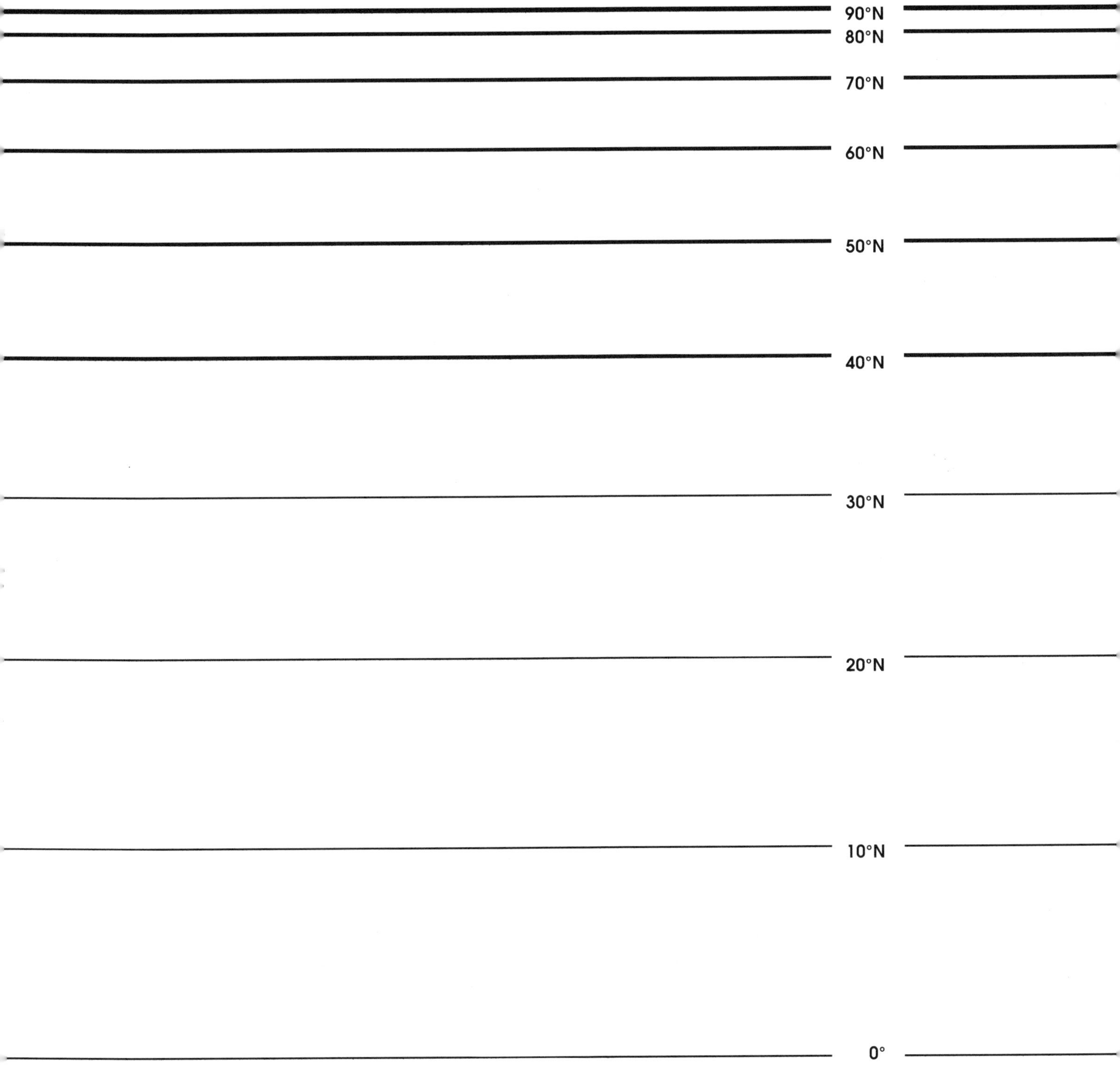

90°N

80°N

70°N

60°N

50°N

40°N

30°N

20°N

10°N

0°

Published by
Princeton Architectural Press
37 East Seventh Street
New York, New York 10003

For a free catalog of books,
call 1.800.722.6657.
Visit our website at www.papress.com.

© 2010 Princeton Architectural Press
All rights reserved
Printed and bound in China
13 12 11 10 4 3 2 1 First edition

Publication of this book has been
supported by a generous contribution from the
Anchorage Museum Foundation.

Editor: Linda Lee
Designer: Erin Kim

Special thanks to: Nettie Aljian,
Bree Anne Apperley, Sara Bader,
Nicola Bednarek, Janet Behning,
Becca Casbon, Carina Cha, Thomas Cho,
Penny (Yuen Pik) Chu, Carolyn Deuschle,
Russell Fernandez, Pete Fitzpatrick,
Wendy Fuller, Jan Haux, Clare Jacobson,
Aileen Kwun, Nancy Eklund Later,
Laurie Manfra, John Myers, Katharine Myers,
Lauren Nelson Packard, Dan Simon,
Andrew Stepanian, Jennifer Thompson,
Paul Wagner, Joseph Weston, and
Deb Wood of Princeton Architectural Press
—Kevin C. Lippert, publisher

Library of Congress
Cataloging-in-Publication Data
Decker, Julie.
Modern north : architecture on the frozen edge /
Julie Decker. — 1st ed.
    p. cm.
 ISBN 978-1-56898-899-3 (alk. paper)
1. Architecture—Arctic regions. 2. Architecture
and climate—Arctic regions. 3. Modern move-
ment (Architecture)—Influence. 4. Architecture,
Modern—20th century. 5. Architecture, Modern—
21st century. I. Title. II. Title: Architecture on the
frozen edge.
NA2542.A72D43 2010
720.911'3—dc22
                                    2009029519

MODERN NORTH

architecture on the frozen edge

Julie Decker

PRINCETON ARCHITECTURAL PRESS | NEW YORK

CONTENTS

PREFACE

An unexpected question came out of developing this publication: What is the North? There isn't always a single, obvious answer. North is sometimes relative—anything not south is north. Other definitions relate the North simply to the characteristic presence of snow and ice. In the context of this publication, the North is defined as the area constituting the circumpolar North, which, if looked at from the top of the globe is the Arctic Ocean surrounded almost completely by a ring of land. The Arctic Circle draws another ring at 66° north latitude; the land above that ring constituting the Arctic and the land just below it the subarctic.

Most of the discussed projects are located within this area, with a few projects below 60° latitude, the line at which we find such notable northern cities as Anchorage and Helsinki. The North presents a building challenges formed by extreme elements and conditions. This is an architecture that, in some way, embraces its latitude—whether reflecting its surroundings, using materials and forms unique to place, or responding in innovative ways to sites unfriendly to modern man.

A review of the selected projects in the book suggests that there is no single contemporary northern style of architecture. But to try to extract one style among such an enormous, perhaps overreaching, geographical scope is likely be too simplistic. Throughout the North, however it is defined, there are hundreds of diverse regions, each with its own indigenous heritage, unique climate, natural environment, and cultural vernacular. It may be fair enough to say that some of these projects could exist anywhere in the world and still be architecturally and aesthetically successful.

Yet each is site-specific, in ways both subtle and obvious. Each architect and firm endeavored to make a building that exists well in its northern condition, within each season, and with each change of light. What stands out in the selection of projects is an architectural response to the North and to the outdoors, whether it is a response to a treeless tundra, mountain base, forest's depth, or glacier's edge. What else remains consistent is a continued interest in the modernist tradition—in buildings that use glass, steel, and concrete within a modern architectural vocabulary, albeit with numerous adaptations to the settings. The projects do not shut out the elements of the North but welcome, embrace, and consider the cultural and climatic conditions and reflect them directly in the buildings' forms and materials. The North is integrated into the modernist principles of building.

There is no one answer to how best to build in such extremes. Solutions are found at each site and pay homage to a variety of traditions, from indigenous houses of the Arctic to the sophisticated building industry of more urban places. There are echoes of cabins and saunas in large-scale public buildings, drawing on the idea of simple structures and materials nestled into natural settings—which can often be enough to create a beautiful building. Many of the buildings would lose their meaning and concept without their particular setting or history.

The architects who designed these projects range from the established to the emerging, from those who have long looked at and worked in the North, to those who brought a fresh eye to the challenges of Arctic entrances, harsh light, and frozen ground. Each designer has taken the building form beyond the utilitarian and beyond the elegant and has integrated the two to create, as a whole, the Modern North.

INTRODUCTION

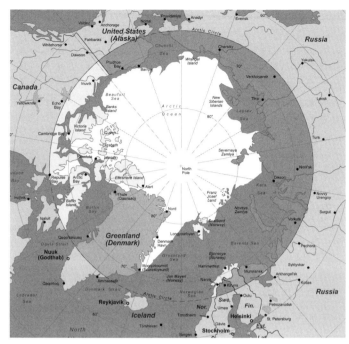

Map of the circumpolar North

In 2008 P.S.1 Contemporary Art Center in Queens, New York, hosted an exhibition of Finnish artwork titled Arctic Hysteria. It portrayed native people living within the Arctic Circle as prone to *piblokto*, or *piboktoq*, loosely translated as "arctic hysteria," with symptoms that include screaming, wild behavior, depression, and insensitivity to extreme cold. Piblokto may have once been caused by vitamin A toxicity, but today it also symbolizes a new interest in the North. Much attention is being paid to winter living today. The declaration of every city north of the equator as a "winter city" to promote tourism and economic development abounds. Cold is hot.

Historically, adventurers have always been drawn to the untarnished lands of the North and to their raw beauty, extraordinary qualities of life, and mystery. Missionaries came to convert the Native populations to Christianity, explorers came on discovery voyages, artists came on junkets—all were interested in conquering and capturing the mystique and telling stories of distant and savage lands upon their return home.

Although the allure of a pristine landscape of the North still remains, today it is oil and climate change that draw the interest up the latitudinal scale. Like the rest of the globe, the North is changing. Scientific evidence shows rapid ice melt in the Arctic, and various political, economic, strategic, and energy issues come into play along with the changes.

Of course, long before curious visitors and settlers migrated to inhabit the North, the indigenous people had learned to live in it. They understood survival in the North. More than that, native northerners knew how to thrive and develop rich cultures based on the place, maintaining a strong spiritual and physical connection to the landscape.

An important part of survival was being able to build structures that would offer protection from the elements. These were utilitarian but ingenious structures built from natural materials that provided shelter from rain, wind, snow, and predatory animals. Each culture across the circumpolar continents devised its own version of the cold-climate dwelling—using snow, ice, wood, and sod. The popular image of the igloo is but one of the many structures. Cold is the greatest threat in the Arctic. To live in it means to find a way to, at times, escape from it.

These temporary and permanent structures of the North were one with the earth, whether they were built above or below the ground. The construction of these shelters required an intimate understanding of wind forces, snow drifting, and other cold-climate physics. Dwellings could be ephemeral and transient, depending on the season and the seasonal activities, or permanent. In the arctic regions of Alaska, the domelike form of the temporary snow structures minimized exposed surface area and maximized structural stability; they warmed quickly, stood up to high winds, and could withstand the weight of a polar bear. When interior warmth would cause the ice to melt, the shape of the dome would force the water to run along the sides of the form and refreeze at the base, thus strengthening the structural system. As new snow fell, another level of insulation from the cold would form. As temperatures increased, the structure would simply melt away, leaving no debris on the land. A more efficient use of materials (and a renewable resource at that) has rarely been seen in the built environment since.

Similarly, the early earth houses of seminomadic cultures, such as *goathe* of the indigenous Sámi culture in Finland, could be temporary or last more than ten years. The sod brick, the building material, eventually melds together and becomes more solid with age. The Sámi have adapted to and flourished above the Arctic Circle, creating building systems using sod brick and other natural materials that went beyond the requirements of survival, with minimal environmental impact. Sámi buildings used the heat generated from interior fires as a key design concept: the buildings were circular in plan, allowing for maximum heat radiation from the centrally located fires.

Architect Ralph Erskine, who earned the nickname "The Arctic Architect of Modernism" after years of work contemplating, designing, and striving to realize an "Ideal Town" north of the Arctic Circle, once said that architecture arises as human beings change the landscape. As human beings began to populate the North, they changed its landscape. As temporary ways of living became permanent, building had to follow.

In the North the climate is made up of short summers and long winters. Summers days are long and light-filled and full of human activity. Winters are dark, with shorter spurts of activity and more time spent indoors. The seasonal rhythm is more extreme than in southern places. There are few transitions; it is full of abrupt, contrasting experiences of warm and cold. Through his study of the relationships between architecture, identity, and the North, Erskine encouraged an architecture that eased the contact between indoors and outdoors. He thought buildings should fit well into the land and consider the way climate affects people.

Buildings of the modern North that were first introduced by settlers, native to the settlers' origins rather than the North, have found ways, often inelegant, to deal with snow, icicles, thawing, and freezing. They are functional. They enclose; they protect. But the North is evolving and growing up, and, so is its architecture. Today, with increasing numbers of designs created by either resident or invited architects for buildings at latitudes climbing above 60 degrees, an opportunity has arisen for a new definition of a northern building, one that is extraordinarily responsive to place and, at the same time, visually provocative.

While there is not a single northern aesthetic to point to—roofs are neither uniformly gabled nor flat, materials are not exclusively natural or man-made—there is a collective knowledge and wisdom that can be used to define northern architecture. It is more than just a building that is constructed in the North. It is northern in the way it responds to the North—the way the architecture mediates the harshness of the low-lying sun without replacing it with the harshness of artificial lights, the way it anticipates snow drifting against the sides, the way it lights up in the darkness, the way it exploits the natural topography and changes the quality of life, and the way it provides visual stimulation in places that sometimes offer little more than an endless expanse of white.

Sometimes it is materiality that ties a building to place—such as Erskine's use of local timbers and birch bark in his 1950s Ski Hotel in Borgafjäll, Sweden. Other times it is the siting, a form growing out of the landscape so that the landscape itself provides shelter from the cold. Sometimes it is the views out of the building and onto the landscape that remind the inhabitant and the visitor of where they are and why it is special. David Chipperfield's design for the new wing of the Anchorage Museum in Alaska, for example, which features a glass facade that feels anything but natural to the surrounding environment, celebrates place in the reflective quality of the glass and the new transparency that allows visitors to view the landscape on the building surface.

These are not all new ideas. Even the ancient Greeks recognized that the winter sun had a low arc in the southern sky—due to the tilt in the Earth—and employed a building technique that allowed windows in the walls to capture much-needed heat from the sun. These buildings were usually built just below the brow of a hill on the southward slope, protected by the hill and by the surrounding shelterbelts of trees. The south face of the building typically contained the main openings to maximize sun exposure. But old or new, it is the specific application of these ideas that creates a distinct identity and, in this case, a new North.

Early settler societies of North America and Canada did not imitate indigenous people's techniques of relating to the environment, including the design and construction of shelters. They instead imported ideas for housing, public buildings, and infrastructure from southern environments. The use of foreign building techniques in the North (but with more insulation) has not led to better northern living. Prototype schools designed for temperate climates and then plopped down in the North for economic efficiency ignore the realities of day-to-day living, of snow piling up in entries and of windows along the north side of a building creating dark, confining spaces.

The projects featured in this publication are more than just structures that exist in the North. From Sami Rintala's design for Hotel Kirkenes, which simplifies and minimizes form to emphasize the vastness and power of the landscape, and Saunders and Wilhelmsen's Aurland Lookout, which propels visitors into the dramatic surroundings, to the village schools of the Yupiit School District designed by Koonce Pfeffer Bettis, whose forms become snow fences, these buildings represent an architecture that responds to the cold, to natural light and extreme conditions, and that is site-specific in its conception. These are not transplanted designs, but embody an approach to understanding and celebrating the unique qualities of the northern latitudes. They offer a way of living that does not isolate man from environment, but unites the North with the north-erner. These projects tell stories that combine isolation with city life, lightness with darkness, tradition with innovation, urbanity with the ultimate grandeur of nature. These buildings contribute significantly to the architectural landscape and the rediscovery of the North.

FLUID GEOGRAPHY

Suddenly…people have come to realize that they can girdle the planet in an infinite number of directions. The world has been surprising itself by coming in…from every unlooked-for direction.
– Buckminster Fuller

Brian Carter

Architect Buckminster Fuller's focus on alternative views of the world and the consequent redefinition of geography that called for a revolution in mapmaking also prompted the consideration of new forms of settlement. More recently, Dr. Joseph Farman's discovery of an ozone hole and the publication of the compelling three-dimensional images of that enormous hole high above the Earth revealed another view of the world and an incentive to revisit the idea of "fluid geography."[1] (Fig. 1)

Other significant shifts have been brought about by global climate change—changes that have impacted both the Arctic and Antarctic. The catastrophic loss of arctic summer sea ice, resulting from global warming, is already transforming the world.[2] Suddenly, places that had previously been remote and isolated have now become accessible. Reports of an unprecedented opening of waters in the Beaufort Sea north of the Yukon/Alaska border, as well as the transformation of the Northwest Passage—an important transpolar route that extends from Baffin Island to the Beaufort Sea south of Victoria Island—into a fully navigable route for the second consecutive year in 2009, underline Fuller's claim of new access from "unlooked-for" directions.[3]

However, Farman's discoveries not only triggered global concern about the depletion of the ozone layer and changes on the surface of the earth but also sparked significant growth in the demand for new types of energy supplies worldwide. This need for alternative sources increased the politicization of energy and prompted an international scramble for new territory that was rich in supplies of oil and gas. Consequently, when a resource-rich seabed in the Far North was discovered, it attracted considerable interest and rekindled an urge to establish settlements in the newly accessible North.

In 1960, after the assertion of a fluid geography, Fuller continued by recommending the need to remap the world using his Dymaxion map, a projection of a world map onto the surface of a polyhedron, which can then be unfolded in many different ways and flattened to form a two-dimensional map. He also suggested a move to "reshape the environment" as an alternative "to reshap(ing) man," which involves the consideration of designs for entire environments rather than isolated individual buildings.[4] And while Fuller's contemporary, philosopher Walter Benjamin, spoke of living in a glass house as the ultimate revolutionary act of an individual, Fuller advocated similar, radical levels of transparency at an urban scale. His development of the geodesic dome as a lightweight, responsive skin that creates an environmental control over domestic spaces also inspired his design study for a two-mile-wide (in diameter) dome covering Manhattan. The dome, which was to extend from the Hudson River to the East River and from Twenty-second Street to Sixty-second Street, was seen as a means to reduce overall energy losses—minimizing requirements for winter heating and summer cooling, obviating the need for snow removal, and making the city more accessible. His proposal was illustrated with an image of a vast transparent dome collaged over New York City. Fuller suggested that "the cost saving in ten years would pay for the dome" and went on to suggest that domed cities are going to be "essential to the occupation of the Arctic and the Antarctic."[5] (Fig. 2)

At about the same time, the engineer Walter Bird was exploring the construction of lightweight, high-performance skins in his designs for new enclosures for radar installations, at the request of the U.S. Air Force. The enclosures would cover the radar installations without impeding their day-to-day operation. His studies addressed the need to construct those installations in remote locations, often in the Far North. This work led to the design and fabrication of air-supported structures, and Bird's designs for the first radomes in the 1950s suddenly made it possible to cover large column-free spaces quickly. The first domes were single-walled structures similar to a child's balloon. Air blowers maintained the dome's shape by creating an interior pressure great enough to support the skin's weight and to withstand wind and snow, while double doors served as an airlock to prevent loss of pressure. By the early fifties hundreds of pneumatic radomes were spread across the tundra as part of North America's early warning defense system. In 1956 Bird founded Birdair Structures to fabricate structures for nonmilitary customers. (Fig. 3)

Bird went on to work on the design of large covered stadiums and, together with the architect Victor Lundy, developed a series of other influential designs in the sixties, including a proposal for a new pavilion for the U.S. Atomic Energy Commission. This design proposed a double-walled, air-supported envelope that enclosed large, column-free spaces; it could be used in different climatic settings. An inflatable structure that required no significant foundation, it could be deflated after use, and easily transported and reerected quickly at another location. Designed in 1960 and fabricated in upstate New York, the portable exhibition hall and theater, with its unique double-breasted profile and bulbous lightweight structure, toured the world for almost a decade. It was described by the critic Reyner Banham as "the vision of a living breathing architecture…never known before."[6] (Fig. 4)

Expo 70 in Osaka, Japan, was arguably the most concentrated collection of lightweight and air-supported structures that covered large open spaces accommodating different functions. The exhibition consisted of a series of expansive spaces, including a 465-foot-long and 275-foot-wide clear span with an air-supported, white-vinyl glass fiber fabric roof created for the U.S. Pavilion. (The fabric was first developed for space suits.) In addition, Festival Plaza, designed by Kenzo Tange, combined a long-span, lightweight frame structure clad with a canopy of cushions made of ETFE (Ethylene tetrafluoroethylene) and filled with air.

Although not formally aligned, Tange later teamed with Bird and architect Frei Otto, and in collaboration with Ted Happold of Ove Arup and Fabwerke Hoechst, they advanced designs for enclosures that covered entire cities. Among these projects was an ambitious scheme to create a new mining community of 45,000 people in the Arctic, which would exist

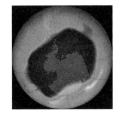

Fig. 1 Hole in ozone shown over Arctic region

Fig. 2 Buckminster Fuller's concept for dome over Manhattan, ca. 1960

Fig. 3 Walter Bird on one of his early Radomes, 1957

Fig. 4 Exhibition building for the Atomic Energy Commission designed by Walter Bird and Victor Lundy, 1960

13

Fig. 5 Jarmund/Vigsnæs, Longyearbyen Research Centre, Svalbard University, Svalbard, Spitzbergen, Norway, 2007

under an air-supported, cable-restrained lightweight roof that spanned 6,500 feet. The proposal offered an alternative to the traditional city.

In 1980 a plan entitled *58 Degrees North* for an enclosed city-in-the-Arctic, commissioned by Syancrude, a Canada-based mining company, advanced that initial proposal. It proposed a new community where ten thousand mine workers would live and work on a remote site near the Athabasca River, almost 110 miles north of Fort McMurray in northern Alberta, Canada—a place that is very cold in winter and hot during the summer. Like Fuller's plan to cover Manhattan, it incorporated a vast, lightweight enclosure that would provide a protected environment where work could continue throughout the year.

Recent designs for new settlements in harsh environments have been inspired by this work. The Khan Shatyr Entertainment Centre, a new center developed by Foster and Partners in Astana, the capital city of Kazakhstan, is located in an austere landscape where winters are long and annual temperatures range between +/-35°C. Kazakhstan is a newly independent country that is rich in oil and gas, and the center was designed and developed to house a range of facilities—shops, restaurants, cinemas, entertainment venues, and car parking—under a vast tent. Enclosed by a skin of ETFE, the new center provides 328,000 square feet of habitable space. The covering of the center is an asymmetrical conical form of a biaxial cable net supported at its apex by a 65-foot-high inverted cone on a 230-foot-tall tripod mast and anchored to the ground. The cable net defines a vast space that is 377 feet wide and 475 feet long. A "world within a world," the center provides a comfortable microclimate and lush landscapes that accommodate a rich mix of uses.[7]

When asked by Svalbard University to design a series of facilities for the new headquarters for the government of Svalbard, on a remote site north of the Arctic Circle in Norway, the Norwegian architecture firm Jarmund/Vigsnaes developed a similar idea: a single vast roof covering a large space under which a range of different facilities can be accommodated. It was completed in 2007. (Fig. 5, see also pages 114–19) However, these designers looked to a unique palette of materials, including a variety of woods and coppers. Longyearbyen, on the Svalbard archipelago, where the headquarters is located, is approximately four hundred miles north of the Norwegian mainland, within a region that straddles the 80° north latitudinal line. Temperatures there range from 20°C in summer to -50°C in winter. Designed to replace a building that had been destroyed by fire in 1996, the sheltered environment for this new seat of the Norwegian government in the region houses government offices, a library, residential accommodation for government officials, a prison, and an emergency rescue control center, all under a vast undulating and folded roof that is clad in preweathered zinc.

Jarmund/Vigsnæs also designed the Svalbard Research Centre (2005), a second building on a nearby site. The design organizes facilities for atmospheric and environmental research, including laboratories, offices, and service facilities, on three levels under a single roof. The form of the expansive, lightweight roof, based on computer simulations, was developed to prevent snow buildup during the winter and to resist extreme weather and strong winds through a variety of angles and slopes. The main structure of the science center is

Fluid Geography

made of wood; the external cladding is copper sheeting, a material that retains its workability even in arctic conditions.

Other designs for new structures in the region respond to the need for more modest facilities in extreme climates. As well as addressing technological needs, these structures are informed by forward-thinking technology but also vernacular building. For example, a Studio Granda–designed single-family house, the Hof Residence, located less than sixty-two miles from the Arctic Circle on the Skagafjörður fjord in Iceland, is an earth-sheltered structure. (Fig. 6, see also pages 140–45) The house is characterized by a heavy structure of wood and concrete, which supports a heavy layer of earth and grass, and clearly benefits from ideas advanced by traditional buildings in the region.

Other projects define a new architecture in harsh environments by exploring industrialized modular construction systems and the development of new materials. The new Halley Research Station, for example, is located on the Brunt Ice Shelf, a particularly inhospitable place off Antarctica's Caird Coast, where temperatures are consistently below 30°C and where heavy blizzards and shifting polar ice are common. Designed for the British Antarctic Survey, one of the world's leading environmental research centers, this new facility replaces a conventional hut-structure station originally built in 1956 on a 500-foot-thick ice shelf. That structure was reinforced and rebuilt several times to cope with heavy annual snowfalls, and Halley IV was finally dismantled in the 1980s.[8] The design for the new facility, by Faber Maunsell and Hugh Broughton Architects in 2004, provides new living spaces, science laboratories, and an energy center for housing generators and other equipment. It consists of a series of prefabricated stilted modules placed on adjustable hydraulic, ski-tipped columns that elevate the living and work spaces above the ground. Consequently, this structure touches the ground lightly. The total budget for the project was almost $80 million and was completed in 2009. The steel-framed structure is clad with reinforced, insulated plastic panels, and the prefabricated units were shipped to the site and reassembled between December and February, the Antarctic summer months. (Fig. 7)

As increasingly energetic international battles are fought over access to newly discovered resources in the Arctic and the Antarctic (an area that the U.S. Geological Survey has estimated may contain as much as 25 percent of the world's untapped oil reserves), there will be an increasing need to design and build settlements, research facilities, and workplaces. The challenges posed by extremely harsh settings, limited building seasons, and recent accessibility offer the potential to inspire a new modern architecture of the North. Developed in response to the need to create spaces that are sophisticated in both appearance and performance, this new architecture of the North prompts fresh engagements with a broad range of ideas that hold the potential to inform ways of living and working as well as the occupation of the land and the design of buildings. As development of these newly "discovered" lands continues, theses global territories are remapped, offering unique design opportunities for architects.

Fig. 6 Studio Granda, Hof Residence, Skagafjördur fjord, Iceland, 2007, view from the west

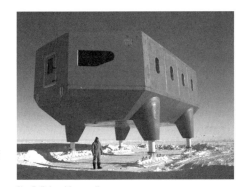

Fig. 7 Faber Maunsell and Hugh Broughton Architects, the new Halley Research Station off Antarctica's Caird Coast designed for the British Antarctic Survey, 2009

The epigraph to this chapter is drawn from Buckminster Fuller, "Fluid Geography," in *Ideas and Integrities: A Spontaneous Autobiographical Disclosure* (Englewood Cliffs, NJ: Prentice-Hall, 1963), 143.

1   Dr. Joseph Farman's discovery and the publication is derived from the Total Ozone Mapping Spectrometer and rendered at NASA's Goddard Space Flight Center.

2   Randy Boswell, "Arctic Rivals Break Ice, Exchange Expertise," *Canwest News Service*, August 10, 2008. This confirmed that the Arctic ice minimum in 2008 would be as extreme as in 2007; between March and September of 2007, almost 9 million square miles of sea ice shrank to a little more than 2 1/2 million. Subsequent predictions prepared by the U.S. National Snow and Ice Data Center were revised.

3   Ibid.

4   R. Buckminster Fuller, "New Forms vs. Reforms," *World*, September 12, 1972, 212.

5   R. Buckminster Fuller, *Utopia or Oblivion: The Prospects for Humanity* (New York: Bantam Books 1969), 353.

6   Reyner Banham, *Age of the Masters: A Personal View of Modern Architecture* (New York: Harper Row, 1962), 89.

7   For more information on this project, see Annette LeCuyer, *ETFE Technology and Design* (Cambridge, MA: Birkhauser, 2008), 138–39.

8   The original hut was called Halley; Halley IV is the fourth structure there.

CONSTRUCTION IN THE COLD

Edwin B. Crittenden

We all know something of winter. We know about the short days and long shadows. But the idea of the North is perhaps more mysterious and less familiar.

Northern regions are defined by their temperature, permafrost, and the Arctic Circle. Regions above the Arctic Circle have alternating seasons of twenty-four hour days of sunlight or of darkness during the year. A mean annual temperature of 32°F often identifies the southern boundary of very cold arctic regions, although this does not give any indication of the extremes of temperature.

The Arctic, which covers a large area, almost equal in size to the entire North American continent, is defined as the land within the Arctic Circle; the subarctic is the land just south of it. They are defined as cold climates primarily by their mean temperatures and the duration of the period during which temperatures stay below 32°F. In the Arctic the mean temperature for the warmest month is -50°F and the average annual temperature is no higher than 32°F. In the subarctic the mean temperature for the coldest month is -32°F, and the mean temperature of the warmest month is above 50°F. Areas of these cold climates in the northern hemisphere include much of Alaska, the northern half of Canada, the Arctic coast of Russia, and the islands of Spitzbergen and Greenland.

The farther north you go, the longer and colder the winters get and the more skill and experience it takes for people to survive. Shelter become important, and it's no surprise that considerations of utility far more than design have defined building in the North. Design and construction criteria as well as the needs of the inhabitants within the Arctic vary. Each location has specific microclimate data and geographic conditions. Although the Arctic may seem like an inhospitable place to live, it encompasses several large cities, including Barrow, Alaska; Tromso, Norway; Murmansk, Russia; and Churchill, Canada. In addition to these cities, there are numerous other large towns and villages; the Arctic Circle and subarctic regions are far from the barren wastelands that are often imagined.

People have inhabited various regions of the Arctic for thousands of years. Humans lived 40,000 years ago in western Siberia, while the earliest presence of humans in North America dates back 15,000 years, when people inhabited Alaska. Researchers believe that Greenland and the Canadian Arctic were settled 11,000 years after Alaska, approximately 4,000 years ago. Many cultures and groups still live in the lands bordering the Arctic Ocean. Among these are the Inuit, Inupiat, and Yup'ik (previously called Eskimos), who range from Alaska to Canada and Greenland; the Sámi (previously called Lapps) of Scandinavia; the Nenets of northwest Russia and the Sakha (Yakut) of Russia; and the Chukchi of Siberia.

Shelters in the Arctic did not take just one form. In prehistoric times, they were built from available resources: snow, ice, wood, sod, and animal hides. Centuries ago, the Inuit used snow houses as temporary structures for shelter as they followed animal herds. The entryways were located in subterranean hallways or tunnels, which prevented heat loss in the main living area and provided storage spaces. A hole in the roof provided ventilation. Seal-oil lamps could keep the temperature constant at 60°F to 70°F. Inuit architecture was based on the principle that warm air rises. Raised sleeping platforms were the warmest part of the

Fig. 1 Typical Arctic sod dwelling in Alaska, 1800s

Fig. 2 Snowdrifts accumulate against and between buildings as snow blows in from the west.

Fig. 3 Snow moves under and between buildings when structures are placed on pilings.

house. Here people rested, ate, and socialized. In summer the majority of people lived in skin tents. Less nomadic members of the family lived in houses framed with driftwood or whalebone, insulated with sod on the outside. (Fig. 1)

The first known contact between European explorers and indigenous groups in North America occurred five hundred years before Columbus. Later, European settlers brought a form of the built environment to the Far North that was unsuited to the severe arctic climate. Their buildings were aboveground post-and-beam structures, built of log and timber. They were energy inefficient, poorly insulated, with no "arctic entries," or no buffer between the cold outdoor air and warm interior space, which created drafts. With World War II, the U.S. and Canadian military introduced prefabricated structures, not dependent upon local resources, to the North. These structures too were ill suited to the cold climate.

Today none of these types of building suffices. The prefabricated box was appropriate to the limitations of transportation and the need for expediency in wartime. The sod home and log cabin were appropriate to a specific time and culture; the temporary snow house, however, is still adequate in an emergency on the open ice. But without a clear, comprehensive understanding of the elements that surround and impact shelters, no structure can provide adequate protection and satisfying habitation in the North.

High winds and blowing and drifting snow can all occur in cold climates. The coastal regions of the Arctic, with few natural buffers, and the open plains of the subarctic are more subject to disturbance by wind than the forested areas south of the tree line. When any object stands relatively isolated in a cold climate, snowdrifts can form on both the windward and the leeward sides. Drifts can reach the height of a building and ultimately extend horizontally to a maximum of ten times the height. Therefore, architectural design in the North often needs to consider not just a single building, but also the critical spacing between buildings. But on the other hand, taking advantage of this collecting of snow, buildings are often erected off the ground to obviate colder or freezing conditions below the building. (Figs. 2 and 3)

Data from the U.S. Centers for Disease Control indicate that extreme cold, rather than heat, is the deadliest form of extreme weather. Certainly, extreme cold is a tremendously inhibiting climatic factor. It demands much from man and equipment, and requires a high level of protection in built environments for human habitation and activities. Just minimizing heat loss can create significant economic and logistical problems in the far north; add in considerations of snow, wind, dry air, frozen ground, and inaccessibility, and any building designer faces a challenge beyond that of aesthetics.

To live in the cold, you need heat. The primary design and construction requirements for facilities in the North are for protection from cold. In order to reflect the demand for energy needed to heat a home or business, heating engineers developed the concept of heating degree days, which relates each day's temperature to the demand for heating fuel. (The heating degree for a particular day is calculated by determining the day's average temperature—the sum of the day's high and low temperatures divided by two. If the resulting

Construction in the Cold

number is above 65°, it is not a degree day. If not, the average temperature is subtracted from 65° to find the number of heating degrees. Cooling degree days follow the same calculation but are related to the energy demands of air conditioning.) The duration of cold in the higher latitudes causes drastic increases in heating requirements. Point Barrow, at the northern tip of Alaska, for example, has a 150 percent increase over Minneapolis.

Factor in windchill, and things get more extreme. A windchill equivalent temperature is often used to describe local weather conditions. A -20°F temperature with a 20-mph wind will produce a windchill factor of -67°F. An experienced and properly clothed person can function normally in windchill temperatures down to -20°F. Windchill factors below that present a serious danger of reducing the ability to perform and freezing exposed flesh.

The importance of minimizing heat loss in buildings is increasingly critical as the heating index—a measurement of the air temperature in relation to the relative humidity, used as an indicator of the perceived temperature—increases. And it is not as simple as turning on the gas. Many areas of the North have long transportation routes; others can only be supplied with fuel once a year by ship or by air. Fuel can become an expensive and precious commodity.

Typically, many prefabricated modules are not adequately insulated from the cold. Without adequate insulation in the walls or windows, condensation in the form of frost builds up on interior surfaces: windows, doorknobs, masonry, and thermal bridges through the wall or roof structures. The high humidity of smaller living spaces for human habitation can be countered by providing adequate exhaust, but this increases heat demand. Ventilated roof structures or cold roofs are advisable to avoid ice-dam damage to insulation caused by the freezing of condensation. (Cold roofs are vented well enough to prevent snow on them from melting when the outside ambient temperature is 22°F or colder. When it is warmer than 22°F, outside melt water usually does not refreeze on cold eaves.)

While the sun might seem a welcome source of light and heat in the Far North, it too poses design challenges. Low sun angles as well as long periods of darkness are characteristic of cold climates. Both are caused by the high latitude and contribute to the low temperatures. North of the Arctic Circle continuous sunlight is received during part or all of the summer, and no sunlight during part or all of the winter. South of the Arctic Circle the sun comes up and goes down daily, with a predictably dark night, despite the season. The sun at Barrow, Alaska, reaches a 43° altitude at noon on its longest day. The sun is 22° above the east horizon at 6 a.m. and the west horizon at 6 p.m., and 3.5° above the northern horizon at midnight. In Minneapolis, Minnesota, the altitude of the noon sun is 68° on June 21st, and 16.5° at 6 a.m. and 6 p.m. There is of course no midnight sun there. (Fig. 4)

Long winter nights and long summer days affect building design primarily in terms of the need to respond to the psychological well-being of the inhabitants. Ideal architectural planning in the North would maximum exposure to the south so that inhabitants could benefit from maximum sunlight. To provide for south-facing exposure, one-story buildings in Alaska can be spaced as close as twenty-five to thirty-four feet apart, whereas in central Canada

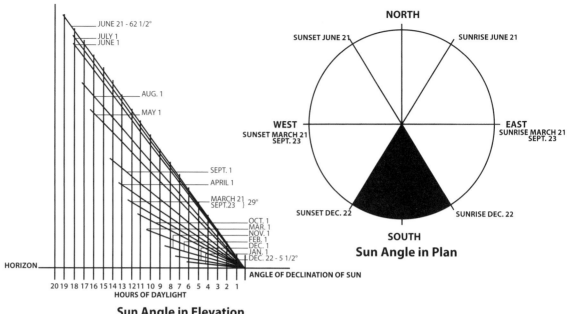

JUNE 21 - 62 1/2°
JULY 1
JUNE 1

AUG. 1

MAY 1

SEPT. 1
APRIL 1
MARCH 21
SEPT.23 } 29°
OCT. 1
MAR. 1
NOV. 1
FEB. 1
DEC. 1
JAN. 1
DEC. 22 - 5 1/2°

HORIZON

20 19 18 17 16 15 14 13 12 11 10 9 8 7 6 5 4 3 2 1
HOURS OF DAYLIGHT

ANGLE OF DECLINATION OF SUN

Sun Angle in Elevation

NORTH

SUNSET JUNE 21   SUNRISE JUNE 21

WEST   EAST
SUNSET MARCH 21   SUNRISE MARCH 21
SEPT. 23   SEPT. 23

SUNSET DEC. 22   SUNRISE DEC. 22

SOUTH
Sun Angle in Plan

Fig. 4 Charting the
Arctic sun: hours of
daylight per month/
season relative to the
angle to the horizon

and farther north, depending on the latitude the sun angles are so low that similar exposure could require spacing buildings 150 to 300 feet apart. In site selection and placing of facilities, a south slope obviously overcomes some of the problems of spacing that will allow sun penetration, and suggests the construction of lower buildings to the south and taller buildings to the north. These site planning factors need to be considered in conjunction with katabatic drift—the flow of air down a slope as it is cooled by radiation—as well as prevailing wind directions and problems of snow drifting.

In the northern summer, residents prefer to be able to allow sunshine to penetrate to the interior by means of strategic placement of windows. To counter the months of darkness and the accompanying feeling of isolation and boredom, interior circulation patterns should maximize human contact, allow views out, and provide for varied architectural spaces and the use of a more vibrant color palette. The long periods of darkness require careful evaluation of the lighting systems, both interior and exterior, to accommodate for a variety of activities as well as privacy.

Snow is perhaps the most obvious element affecting construction in the Far North, although it has considerably less impact than in the more moderate coastal zones farther south. With careful planning, snow can be used as insulation around foundations, banked against the north side of buildings, and even held on roofs through "snow catchers" to prevent snow falling onto undesired places. But windblown, dry, fine snow can penetrate the most minute cracks or openings.

Furthermore, the long duration of snow cover emphasizes the remoteness and isolation of the North, and a barren, monotonous landscape, with its solitude and silence, can have psychological effects. The often flat environment distorts perspective and judgment of distances. The uniformity of color and forms that are leveled out by drifting snow emphasizes the bleakness. Whiteout and ice fog conditions near the ground can, even on otherwise perfectly clear days, wipe out all sense of scale and distance. On the other hand, the landscape of the Arctic and the effect of the low sun angles can be extremely beautiful.

The snow in the North is often blowing snow. Wind whips through the landscape, moving snow and howling through any openings in both natural and man-made structures. It can be a commanding force. Wind speeds and directions in both winter and summer are affected by the topography; in flatter areas, wind directions are relatively constant and can be uniform in force. To accommodate for this, the architect must consider the windchill factor, heat loss, and snow drifting in structural requirements. On the other hand, the arrangement of structures can also influence wind patterns—either positively or negatively—in the microconditions of a small northern community. When wind speeds near the ground are approximately seven to ten miles per hour, fresh snow particles can be picked up and carried along over smooth surfaces until they are deposited in any area where the wind speed is reduced by interaction with an object, such as a building.

Consideration of major access routes, pedestrian walkways, and building exits typically has priority in planning for conditions of drifting snow and wind. Wind, when funneled between buildings or forced through a narrow space, can develop considerable force and become a serious problem. Upwind barriers, such as snow fences or a line of buildings, can provide some control by collecting drifts. Minimizing the building area that is perpendicular to the wind will reduce heat loss and drifting. This orientation must be weighed against positioning desirable for other reasons, such as access, provision of views, and sunshine. An aerodynamic shape with rounded or diagonal corners, both vertical and horizontal, helps reduce turbulence and decreases the impact of high winds. Wind, which can penetrate cracks around the windows, doors, and other openings, increases heat loss. On the leeward side, specifically, high winds can draw warm air out of buildings though crevices and openings. Triple-glazed sashes and the use of modern sealants and caulking significantly help mitigate this loss.

While the snow and wind swirl above ground, the cold penetrates much deeper at times. Permafrost and deep frost layers are the least understood and perhaps most significant special conditions of some cold-climatic regions. About one-half of the land area of Canada and Russia, more than 60 percent of Alaska, 22 percent of China, and most of Greenland and Antarctica are underlaid by perennially frozen ground—more commonly known as permafrost. Permafrost is also encountered in isolated locations near lakes and streams at high elevations, and in shaded and extremely wet locations considerably farther south.

Fig. 5 Placement of buildings on pilings or on above ground foundations mitigates the destruction of the building due to permafrost.

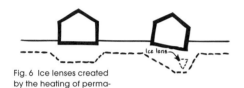

Fig. 6 Ice lenses created by the heating of permafrost can cause buildings and foundations to sink.

There are many types and conditions of permafrost, which occurs where the thermal condition in soil or rock is persistently below 32°F. Continuous permafrost is that which occurs without thaw throughout a large region. Discontinuous permafrost is that which occurs in some areas while other areas are free of it.

The amount of ice present in permafrost may vary from a small number of minute particles to as much as 90 percent, depending on the location and the season. Permafrost forms a layer impervious to moisture and all water from rain and snow that accumulates above. This accounts for the swampy characteristics of the northern tundra in the summertime, since the ground cannot absorb the water. The vegetation of the tundra forms an insulating blanket that effectively maintains a small active layer of soil generally less than three feet thick. Disturbance of that mat of vegetation increases thaw rates, raises soil temperatures, and causes the permafrost to melt, thus altering the character of the surface.

Since permafrost is a phenomenon of temperature, any change in the thermal regime of an area can lead to thawing, resulting in a topography of mounds, sinkholes, caverns, and ravines. Man-made disruption of the natural regime seriously affects the delicate thermal equilibrium. Cleaning, digging of trenches, and erection of buildings may result in the thawing of the frozen ground or even the raising of the permafrost table. A mechanical problem associated with the degradation of permafrost is that, upon thawing, the ground material may lose its capacity to support a heavy structure placed atop it.

The soil overlying permafrost—the level of annual frost or the active layer that freezes and thaws seasonally—can vary in depth from as little as several feet in the far north to ten or twelve feet in sporadic permafrost zones. Because ice crystals take more space than liquid water, this active layer often causes frost heaving as the temperature changes, and can result in serious damage to foundations and buildings. There are numerous examples of buildings settling with their floor levels well below the original ground surface, and other cases are where the building is completely destroyed.

In the extreme north, where the permafrost is stable and there is a minimal active layer, many structures are built on piles driven or thawed into permafrost and shaped or banded to avoid uplift. Only the piles and the utility connections transmit heat to the frozen ground, and buildings separated from the ground by piles usually do not degrade the permafrost. Recent developments of thermal or heat valves—usually tubes filled with gas or liquid—allow withdrawal of heat from the underlying soils and radiating it to the atmosphere. Newer systems use smaller pipes called thermaprobes, which can be placed alongside foundations or piles, placed horizontally under the slab and foundation, or even driven in later on as a means of repair to achieve the same goal. (Figs. 5 and 6)

As thawing poses challenges, so does the threat of frozen pipes. Adequate utilities in cold climates are often the most difficult and costly to construct and maintain. Water supplies for domestic use and for fire protection, and for waste and sewage disposal systems must be protected from low temperatures. Individual wells and septic tanks are generally prohibited by the presence of permafrost or by deep seasonal frost up to twelve feet. Conventionally piped

Construction in the Cold

water supplies and sewage systems in unheated and uninsulated pipes buried in permafrost quickly freeze. Service lines can be placed on or above the ground surface in insulated arctic pipes, but even prefabricated arctic pipes with foam insulation and a protective metal skin that are supported above ground are exposed to damage. An alternative is insulated and heated pipes in utilidors, which are insulated conduits that house water, wastewater, and sewage pipes, and in some instances, steam or hot water lines for heating, and electric and communication system distribution. They may be made of wood as an insulated box, or of insulated metal panels and placed directly on the ground or raised high enough for passage below. Heating of the utilidors is achieved by supplying heat to the air within the utilidor, by heating the water that is circulated, or by electric heat tracing. Insulation not only protects the waterlines from freezing, but also the permafrost from thawing.

Reservoir construction in the Arctic is an expensive operation, but it is often necessary where natural water supply storage is not adequate. Lakes are the usual source of water if the depth is great enough to provide water below the winter ice. Wells can be used in areas where water strata can be found below the permafrost. Water can be distributed in three general ways within arctic communities: by tank trucks, by summer piping systems supplemented by cold-water tank truck delivery, and by waterlines in insulated utilidors.

Utilities only work with power. Power generation and distribution can be critical from a life safety point of view. In extreme cold, a breakdown of power sources for periods of even an hour or two can be disastrous. Generation and distribution systems differ only slightly in cold climates from those in more moderate zones. However, the cost of fuel and the need to replace equipment in order to avoid lengthy shutdowns increases operating and maintenance costs. Waste heat from generation units is commonly reused in heating systems. Electrical power requirements are considerably higher on a per capita basis due to the increased lighting demands and use of electrical heat in remote locations where normal utility service and heating would be difficult and expensive.

Keeping a building warm and functional also means considering humidity and ventilation. In extreme cold, the use of operable windows is discouraged. Closed storm vestibules (arctic entries) are provided to reduce vapor condensation that can build up on doorframes, freezing them shut or forcing off the hinges. Arctic entries also provide personal protection and reduce heat losses. Equipment such as heating, ventilating, and air conditioning (HVAC) units and exhaust fans cannot be placed in exposed locations because of the extreme temperature differences to which the equipment would be exposed, particularly if it is on a controlled cycle with nightly shutdown. Outside air intakes and exhaust outlets require baffles to trap the windblown snow, preventing it from entering into the ductwork or thawing and causing leaks.

Many other factors in addition to the harsh climate and the remoteness of development sites contribute to the high cost of construction in the North. Lack of skilled local labor plays a significant role in escalating total costs. Mechanical design and controls should be as simple and maintenance-free as possible, since labor forces generally are not familiar with more complicated systems. Because of the limited size of communities and the small number of people in them, contractors often need to recruit employees from elsewhere and furnish living accommodations for them. These structures are usually portable, temporary, and small, with limited recreational facilities. Governments and trade unions have set minimum standards for camp facilities.

The high cost of manpower also includes termination cost due to seasonal and cyclical fluctuations in employment and the lower productivity rate compared to that in temperate-zone working areas. Physical productivity is reduced for a variety of reasons: adverse climate, psychological stress, use of construction methods and equipment unsuitable for arctic conditions. This reduction of productivity can mean an increase in labor costs from 33 to 50 percent for winter construction. Isolation and extreme working conditions are the most frequent causes of labor-force turnover.

One of the most frustrating problems is maintaining optimum inventories of materials. Careful planning and good logistical control are required to ensure that materials are at the site when needed, but not stored any longer than necessary. Construction materials and stored equipment, both during shipment to the job site and while in storage, need to be protected. Damage in transit not only raises costs but can also result in a shortage of the materials or equipment needed at a crucial time.

The most common methods of handling construction material and equipment in transit and on the job site are palletization and containerization. The pallets and containers are limited to a size that the available equipment can handle. Unfortunately, material wastage sometimes increases from a norm of 5 percent to 15 or 20 percent. Construction equipment must be modified to protect it from temperature-related failure and to protect the operator from weather extremes. Extreme subzero temperatures place a heavy burden upon operating equipment; long idle times increase the need for engine overhaul; tires become brittle from cold; the climate amplifies metal and hydraulic-systems failure—all of these significantly reducing its life expectancy.

Another problem of maintaining equipment at remote job sites centers around replacing parts and providing special-purpose tools. Whenever possible, equipment with identical component parts that require a smaller overall inventory of repair parts (for example, engines and hydraulic systems) is used. Standby equipment is often supplied because of the difficulty of obtaining service and parts. As a result, tying job productivity to single-purpose equipment, even if this seems more efficient, is a practice to be avoided.

Transportation of construction materials and other supplies to arctic sites is often the determining factor in the final cost of the project. Delivery of materials can be accomplished by marine, land, or air transportation. At times, more than one of these methods may be necessary, but not necessarily available year-round. In Alaska, for example, materials for the development of oil-drilling facilities at Prudhoe Bay were shipped to the small coastal town of Seward in southcentral Alaska, freighted to Fairbanks in the interior of the state by train, and then trucked north to Prudhoe Bay over ice roads in the winter or air freighted in the summer.

Because of seasonal ice conditions and shallow near-shore waters, marine transportation to the Arctic is limited. The ocean route around Point Barrow, Alaska, for example, is open for only six weeks, during August and September. Road transport, too, is extremely limited. Except for the trans-Alaska pipeline's "haul road," which was used for transporting supplies from the interior to the state's north-shore oil fields, there are no overland routes to the Arctic in Alaska, although snowmobiles and tractor trains can be used for travel in winter. In summer, heavy equipment can seriously damage the very sensitive tundra with its thawed soils and standing water. This effectively prohibits overland travel in summer except on foot.

Thus, air transportation plays a major role in arctic activities. Aircraft can operate year-round and provide the fastest means of transporting supplies. To inland communities, air is often the only means of freight transportation. Most villages however have only minimal internal road systems connecting them with their airstrips.

At times, the more efficient and economical construction method is to build off-site. The oil-gathering stations, as well as the oil operations center at Prudhoe Bay on the northern coast of Alaska, were completely fabricated in the continental United States. They were barged in on maximum-sized modules to the North Slope, where, with a minimum crew, the modules were carried on crawlers to the site and jacked onto pilings. Over the past years, a large percentage of the construction projects in Greenland were prefabricated in Denmark. Much of the housing in the Canadian eastern Arctic is prefabricated in the south and shipped to various locations for erection. Post-WWII housing in Bethel, Alaska, a village accessible only by air or water, was completely fabricated on an enclosed ship in the community and skidded to location. Whether prefabricated or built on-site, however, the challenges associated with building in the North are more than construction related. Good design also considers the psychological impacts of northern living. The high latitude, with its long summer days and winter nights, is disruptive to the typical waking and sleeping patterns of people. Long periods of extreme cold slow down or halt outdoor activity and motivation, increase the feeling of isolation and confinement, and create a need for vigilance to maintain personal and facility safety.

Looking to indigenous ways of life may provide insights to building in the North. Native communities were traditionally small, often consisting of a single-family group. They were in balance with the ecology and natural food supply. Villages were far apart and located near hunting grounds. Overpopulation meant starvation, as did disruption of the natural environment. The scarcity of materials for building and the climate resulted in minimal-sized structures, often partially below ground and, in winter, generally covered with snow.

Social, psychological, and economic needs of southern culture transposed into the North have created a major conflict between the indigenous people and outsiders. Most native communities today still cling to some of the social and subsistence structure of their culture, but are dependent on the social and economic structure of southern culture: the introduction of social services, transportation means, and a monetary economic base. Some of the change has been gradual, through early contact with whalers, freighters, miners, missionaries, and government officials. For many, however, the shift has been rapid, starting with contact with the U.S. military in World War II in Alaska, and now with today's oil and gas exploration. Schools and community centers have been built with government funds and imported labor. Sewage and water systems have been provided, not just to communities, but also to individual homes. Food and other provisions are available at community stores. Throughout the North, technological response to physical conditions has been rapid. In the United States, the military, oil and gas companies, and federal and state governments provide facilities with standards nearly equal to those provided in the south. The cash economy is there, and the younger generations are making the shift, by and large, to Western culture.

Contemporary designers of arctic and subarctic facilities have recognized the need for more complete analysis of social and psychological requirements for living in the North. And they realize that economical solutions should not mean sacrificing functional livability. A design philosophy is required that concentrates quality life-support systems for a healthy and consistent interior climate; includes a variety of spaces, volumes, shapes, textures, and colors of materials to provide relief from the monotony of the surrounding environment; and offers both a physical and visual sense of full protection from the exterior climate.

Many years ago, Yonnie Fischer, a young student at the University of Alaska in Fairbanks, Alaska, drew a concept for the North after her father had returned from a conference on northern design. She described the concept behind the drawing as:

Fig. 7 Yonnie Fischer, Illustration of the northern-city concept

A nice, old gentleman lived somewhere north of the Yukon. He had a dog and loved to roam the country. One day the government told him of big things. They were going to build a big dam and a fine domed city for all the people displaced. This they did and required all to move into this fabulous place (no dogs allowed). It was beautiful with palm tress and piped sweet music. The gentleman visited the shiny complex, but was very unhappy. He moved out, found his dog, found an old log cabin by a lake and lived happily ever after. (Fig. 7)

Contemporary designers in the North face a challenge both old and new—to create facilities to be used and enjoyed by, as well as to protect, man. A building's orientation, its openings, its skin, and its systems can protect from the natural environment but also be inspired by it. The northern architect explores the possibilities for a unique northern aesthetic, as meaningful to place as the indigenous structures, using a contemporary understanding and technology to create an architecture that does more than simply provide shelter.

THE NORTHERN DIMENSION: BETWEEN UNIVERSALITY AND LOCALITY

Juhani Pallasmaa

THE POWER OF PLACE

Architecture mediates between culture, nature, landscape, and the continuum of time. It is molded in the context of landscape—both natural and man-made—but it is also a dialogue with history and tradition, and it acquires its very meaning from these contextual framings. Yet we tend to underestimate the significance of place in the formation of human character, behavior and thought, architecture and cities, and vice versa, the impact of our internal mental landscape on our constructed world.[1]

Edward T. Hall, the American anthropologist, whose books open seminal insights into the cultural specificity of behavior and the human use of and interaction with space as the unconscious prerequisites of architecture, points out our regrettably weak capacity to acknowledge and read the language of environments, spaces, and objects, and their impacts on our lives.[2]

> The most pervasive and important assumption, a cornerstone in the edifice of Western thought, is one that lies hidden from our consciousness and has to do with a person's relationship to his or her environment. Quite simply, the Western view is that human processes, particularly behavior, are independent of environmental controls and influence.[3]

The writer here points out the secret conditioning of buildings is based in human behavior, but the natural geographic and climatic conditions, in fact, even have a double impact: first directly upon culture and behavior; and second, through architecture that has been adapted to these primary causalities.

As cultural geography has established, landscape is read in metaphorical terms, and we project a strong correspondence between our bodies and the landscape: the landscape is interpreted as a metaphorical body and the body as a metaphorical landscape. Consequently, landscape and climate are not merely contexts of human existence, they structure human character, experience, and processes of thought.

We tend to regard buildings as mere aestheticized physical objects and forget that they exist simultaneously in physical and natural as well as mental and cultural spheres, and that they structure and direct feelings, thoughts, and behavior. Architecture is always also mental space, and it provides our most important horizons of experiencing and understanding the world and, essentially, ourselves.

UNIFICATION AND DIFFERENTIATION

The differing architectures of various climate conditions, landscapes, and cultural traditions surely echo these primary existential conditions. Until the beginning of the industrial age, northern building traditions directly reflected their physical contexts. This close interdependence gave rise to numerous unique building cultures around the world, ranging from the constructions of the Alaskan Indian and Eskimo cultures to the ancient Icelandic stone structures and the peat chambers and mobile huts of the nomadic Lapps of northern Scandinavia, Finland, and Russia. The most characteristic building tradition of the northern forest region is, of course, the horizontal log structure that was even transferred to the North American continent during the early immigration phase. The early forms of human settlement in the North were frequently nomadic due to the need to cover a vast area of land in order to secure a livelihood. Among the survival cultures of cold climates and scarcity, construction was naturally based on locally available materials, ranging from earth and stone to wood, whalebones, animal skins, and snow.

However, the universalizing impact of industrial technology has gradually weakened the interdependence of building and locality, and consequently the identities of Nordic traditions. In its dream of universal technologized culture, the modern utopia of the past two centuries has almost entirely detached human dwelling and architecture from their ties with locality. Authentic regional characteristics, arising from necessity, have often degenerated into shallow thematized architectures and sentimental consumerist kitsch. Regardless of this industrial development, a Nordic ambience continues to be recognizable in architecture, although in a more subdued manner. Yet local identity and specificity should not be romanticized, but rather seen as products of often conflicting historical processes, influences, and aspirations.

Architecture takes place at the intersection of tradition and innovation, convention and uniqueness, practicality and belief, collectivity and individuality, past and present. In the Nordic cultures, architecture—and particularly modernist architecture—has become firmly rooted in the society, and during the past century, architecture was guided by its determined social mission. The art of building had been seen and used as a means of societal reaffirmation, unification, and solidarity rather than of differentiation and social separation.

The traditional ethnic, cultural, and social homogeneity of each of the Nordic cultures, as well as the relatively long periods of undisrupted social and economic development, have created a sense of coherence and collective responsibility. This social history is, naturally, reflected in architecture and gives it a sense of stability and purpose.

Even in today's era of global consumerism and universal aesthetic fashions, a Nordic sensibility and architectural culture are distinguishable from, say, those of Central Europe, the Mediterranean, or North America. Yet the differences between the various Nordic cultures are as distinct as their similarities, although these characteristics are difficult to describe. It is not easy to explain in words how a Swedish or Norwegian building differs from a Finnish one, but the difference is intuitively and unconsciously recognizable at first sight.

Environmental perceptions and reactions synthesize an incredible amount of ingredients, and language does not seem to be adequate to describe cultural and embodied phenomena, such as the interactions of natural environment and building culture. Architecture and human settlements are materializations of entire cultures, and they contain more messages than can be told in words. Culture weaves together an endless array of physical conditions, conscious and unconscious behavioral features, collective responses, values, beliefs, and images, which are materialized in our physical settings and architecture.

MATERIAL AND MENTAL CONTEXTS

Indigenous and vernacular building traditions anywhere in the world are generally closely tied to prevailing local conditions, such as landscape and topography, climatic and soil conditions, available materials and local crafts. In traditional northern buildings, the cold temperature and the presence of snow are inevitably reflected in the heavy and insulating wall and roof structures and steep roof forms, such as in the ancient *stave* churches of Norway, Finnish medieval churches, and the generally closed and protective image of Nordic farm buildings. The oldest buildings of the North, such as ancient stone and turf structures or farmhouses built of wood, are tied to their settings through materials that derive directly from the land and integrate them with the textures and coloration of their settings. (Fig. 1)

Yet, as author and environmental behaviorist Amos Rapoport argues, physical determinism fails to explain the specificity of built forms, as they are fundamentally determined by sociocultural and mental factors.[4] The decisive role of cultural factors arises from the fact that buildings are not solely rationally constructed shelters against the threats of the physical world; they are also mental and metaphysical constructions that reflect the existential sphere of traditions, myths, beliefs, and ideals.

Vernacular construction is closely tied to the continuum of tradition, which allows for only a limited margin of individual expression. As stylistic and aesthetic choices eventually gain importance, the self-conscious aspirations of individualistic designers tend to detach architecture from its dependence on guiding and unifying principles, and formal ideals tend to become detached from the realities of place and time.

The persistence of the classical idiom and its repeated reemergence throughout history illustrates the role of universal ideals. The first consciously applied national architectural styles in Nordic countries were the various neoclassical styles of the eighteenth and nineteenth centuries. Classical elements were echoed even in modest peasant buildings. Furthermore, in the late seventeenth and early eighteenth centuries, most Nordic towns, which had grown rather spontaneously until then, were replanned according to Renaissance classical principles, and town houses were built, primarily of wood, in local variations of classicism.

THE EVOLUTION OF NORDIC MODERNITY

The romantic movements of the end of the nineteenth century sought explicitly to re-create local and national styles on the basis of indigenous historical precedents, and architecture was deliberately used to strengthen national identities. However, the artistic products often ended up following concurrent continental European, or even more distant, trends. As a consequence of such conflicting ideals, in Finland, for instance, the buildings of Eliel Saarinen and his two partners, Hermann Gesellius and Armas Lindgren, echo precedents from the urbanized continent and even the American Midwest more than any indigenous examples.

The next impact of external influence came barely two decades later, in the midcentury. The delightfully spirited neoclassicist architecture of the 1920s Nordic classicist period

Fig. 1 Tyrvää Church, Vammala, Finland, early sixteenth century. A medieval Finnish church with its characteristic steep roof.

Fig. 2 Alvar Aalto, Town hall, Kiruna, Finland, 1958, competition entry. The shape of the building mirrors the profile of the adjacent artificial mounds of mining slag. The northern facade is almost entirely closed as a protection against cold winds.

Fig. 3 Alvar Aalto, Lappia Theatre and Radio Building, Rovaniemi, Finland, 1969–70/1970–75. The roofscape echoes the profiles of the mountain landscape around the city.

was inspired by *architettura minore*, the anonymous urban vernacular of northern Italy. Nordic architects followed Mediterranean ideals, to the degree that in the mid-1920s Alvar Aalto (1898–1976) aspired to turn his humble hometown of Jyväskylä in central Finland, built at the time mainly of one- and two-story wooden buildings, into "northern Florence."[5]

The reductive expression of Nordic classicism paved the way for the emergence of functionalism in the late 1920s. As the formal simplicity of the new architecture was close to the ageless traditions of peasant buildings and also appealed to the Nordic Protestant mentality in its asceticism, modernity became accepted more widely and quickly in Scandinavia than elsewhere.

Modernist architecture tended to underrate the local climate in its tendency to follow ideals deriving from Europe south of Scandinavia. It is quite revealing that ever since the beginnings of modernity, architects have surrounded their buildings in their drawings with lush deciduous trees and rarely showed coniferous trees that dominate the Nordic landscape. The modernist flat roofs, vulnerable materials, and large glass surfaces could not have been motivated by the physical and climatic realities of the North. The modern tendency to regard structures as contrasts to the prevailing landscape and tradition further reinforced the detachment of architecture from the specific characteristics of place.

Regardless of these general characteristics, Nordic modern and contemporary architectures have their distinct identities among the architectural cultures of the modern world, and they have widely been regarded as exemplary of architecture's ability to be rooted in its physical and cultural reality. Nordic modernity is generally characterized by a human scale, subtle interplay with nature, preference for natural materials and crafts, sense of democracy, modesty, and formal understatement. Instead of an abrupt break with tradition, a feeling of uninterrupted continuity from indigenous and earlier historical styles to contemporary architecture can usually also be felt. Due to what became the deep association of Nordic societies with ideas and ideals of modernity, the widely popular postmodernist trend of the 1980s left few traces in the architecture of the northern countries.

MOTIFS OF THE NORTH

As Nordic architectures are often given as examples of locally adapted, or situated, modern architecture, it is surprising that since the emergence of modernity there have been remarkably few cases of grounding a formal architectural language on specifically Nordic conditions. Local and cultural identity seems rather to arise unconsciously and diffusely, and without conscious intentions.

A Nordic ambience can easily be sensed in the buildings of Aalto, for instance, although they may not contain any explicit motifs of the North. Yet some of Aalto's buildings, such as his project (1958) for the city hall of Kiruna, a mining town in Sweden, and his Lappia House (1969–76) in Rovaniemi, Finland, in Lapland, deliberately mimic landscape forms of the area: in the first case, the mounds of mining slag surrounding the site, and in the latter case, the contours of the fields outside the city. (Figs. 2 and 3) Aalto's frequent use of undulating sculptural shapes is often seen as a direct reference to features of Finnish lake landscapes.[6] His architectural masterpiece, Villa Mairea (1938–39), in Noormarkku, Finland, weaves together images of international modernism and motifs of Finnish vernacular tradition, and creates a moving counterpoint between architectural and forest space.[7] (Fig. 4)

Fig. 4 Nordic "forest space." Alvar Aalto, Villa Mairea, Noormarkku, Finland, 1938–39. Entrance hall, living room, and main stairway.

A strong sense of locality arising from reflections of northern landscape and vernacular traditions—the severe climatic conditions in terms of snow, wind, and requirements for efficient thermal insulation—is evident in various projects of Ralph Erskine (1914–2005), who was born and educated in Great Britain but settled to work in Sweden. Early on in his career, he made studies of the use of snow as an insulating material and a means of wind protection. He also developed ways of eliminating heat transfer through structural elements extended through external walls, by means of suspending balconies of apartment buildings from above on the facade. His Tourist Hotel in Borgafjäll (1948) with its pitched and sloping roofs and integration of building volumes with shaped terrain, as well as the rustic interior spaces, is expressive of a northern genius loci.

Erskine also combined highly technological projects with a northern regional character. His dome-shaped Villa Engström on Lisö Island (1955–56), for example, makes one think of Eskimo igloos and Buckminster Fuller's slightly earlier Wichita House (1946).

Erskine's residential buildings of the early 1960s in Kiruna and Svappavaara in northern Sweden, with their rounded corners and hill-like sectional profiles, acknowledge wind forces and simultaneously project an imagery adopted to the context of the *fjeld* (a high, barren plateau) landscape. His large-scale buildings for Stockholm University in the 1980s, with their folded roof shapes and projecting eaves, create a distant echo of vernacular farm and industrial buildings.

After a short phase of formal abstraction in his youth, Reima Pietilä (1923–93), in collaboration with his wife, Raili (b. 1926), sought to develop a specifically local modern architectural language through morphological studies of Finnish landscape types. The Dipoli Student Union (1961–66) in Otaniemi arises from the bedrock and is partly covered by huge blocks of granite from the site. His project for the Finnish Embassy (1963, 1983–85) in New Delhi, India, projects topological images of Finnish lake landscapes, whereas the residence of the president of the Republic (1983, 1985–87) in Helsinki derives from studies of Nordic geology. The unexecuted project for the Malmi Church (1967) in Helsinki is like an immense cliff formation.

The Norwegian Sverre Fehn's (1924–2009) projects are always strongly tied to their soil, and they are set in a dialogue with their settings, from the characteristics of the terrain and landscape to the vegetation. Some of Fehn's projects, such as the unexecuted project for an art gallery, Verdens Ende (1988), the Glacier Museum (1991) in Fjaerland, and Villa Busk (1987–90) in Bamble, are engaged in powerful and poetic dialogues with their extraordinary sites. The forceful concrete and wood structures of the Hedemark Museum (1979) in Hamar reflect both vernacular Norwegian traditions and the twelfth-century ruins that the building encloses.

Juhani Pallasmaa   31

Fig. 5 Matti Sanaksenaho, St. Henry's Ecumenical Art Chapel, Turku, 1995/2005. The building is an example of today's aspiration for a tradition-bound Nordic expression away from international technological rationalism.

Remarkably, even the formally reductivist works of the North, from Arne Jacobsen's elegant modernism to today's minimalists, convey a sense of distinct place through their sense of well-articulated scale, haptic materiality, careful detailing and execution, and an interplay with their sites. An authentic and assuring sense of place and rootedness arises unconsciously and unintentionally from numerous minute and almost unnoticeable choices, reflexes, and sensibilities rather than conscious intentions and programmatic formal themes and motifs. A genuine sense of local specificity reflects internalized and embodied (rather than intellectualized) characteristics of landscape and culture.

LYRICAL PRAGMATISM

The peasant mode of life and a rural sense of propriety are still present in the Nordic psyche, especially in Finland, creating a type of split personality suspended between the rural and urban modes of life. In the summer, most Finns relocate to their summer huts, rejecting the comforts of technology, of urban life, for the lifestyle of the primordial forest dweller. During those summer weeks, Finns have different approaches to life than during the long winter months lived in cities. The architecture of Nordic summer houses designed since the beginnings of modernity, such as Knut Knutsen's own rugged summer house (1961) and Wenche Selmer's delightfully traditionalist vacation houses (1960s–1980s) in Norway (which make one think of the icons of domesticity in the paintings of Carl Larsson), often expresses a return to the ageless farm building. Icelanders and Norwegians move to their solitary huts in the mountains in their spare time, whereas Swedish summer dwelling tends to be less primitive, more cultured and social.

The sense of societal purpose, since the late nineteenth century, has given rise to an attitude of social responsibility as opposed to artistic self-expression, and has led to an emphasis on functional and technical practicalities over artistically autonomous or utopian aspirations. A functionalist ethic still prevails in Nordic architecture today. The societies are tradition-bound in that the strong connection to society suppresses extreme individualistic tendencies. Even personal expression tends to acknowledge the boundaries of the accepted collective canon. Moderation, temperance, and restraint are widely regarded as virtues in social behavior as well as in art, design, and architecture. The combined attachment to nature and an unpretentious practicality give rise to an architecture of lyrical pragmatism in opposition to the stylized and aestheticized architecture celebrated today. (Fig. 5, see also pages 68–75)

NORDIC LIGHT

Some years ago I saw an exhibition of Nordic painting of the turn of the century entitled The Northern Light at the Reina Sofia Museum in Madrid. The paintings were hung thematically, irrespective of their country of origin. I was struck by the uniformity of feeling—the Nordic ambience—in the artworks: scenes of human figures in landscapes, dim dusk and twilight, a sensation of humility and silence, and a distinct sense of melancholy. I sensed a familiar

The Northern Dimension: Between Universality and Locality

silence, matter-of-factness, sobriety, and a tangible sense of reality. There was no discrepancy between appearances and essences in this world of solitude and tranquility.

The singularity of the Nordic sensibility was unexpectedly revealed by the sharpness of the southern light and the urbane bustle of Spanish life in the streets around the museum. I had not grasped this unity quite so clearly before this encounter. The same experience would certainly arise if a collection of Nordic buildings could be similarly placed within a southern context.

In the severe climate of the North, where light is precious, it may enter buildings from below, reflected by water or snow. Light is an essential quality of life and architecture. The extreme contrasts of the seasons, the extended days in midsummer and the almost constant darkness in midwinter, all sensitize people to light and its surprising variations. Light is a delight and gift. Although Nordic architecture is often praised for a sensitive articulation of light, uses of daylight have usually been rather spontaneous. Only during the past few decades has light gained importance as a conscious architectural design intention.[8]

The undisputed master of light in modern architecture is Aalto. Throughout his career he developed countless ways of articulating natural light: from the cylindrical skylights of the Viipuri Municipal Library (1927–35) in Vyborg, Russia, the huge double-layered glass prisms of the National Pensions Institute (1948, 1952–57) in Helsinki, and the superb instruments of light in the Church of the Three Crosses (1955–58) in Vuoksenniska, Finland, to the complex skylighting systems of the Helsinki University of Technology (1949, 1953–56) in Otaniemi and the North Jutland Museum (1958, 1966–72) in Aalborg, Denmark. Whereas Aalto's buildings are celebrations of the soft light of the North, the two churches of Sigurd Lewerentz (1885–1975), St Mark's Church in Björkhagen, Stockholm (1956–60) and St. Peter's Church in Klippan, Sweden (1963–66), are both primarily based on the calming interpretation of shadow and darkness, the other dramatic light condition of the northern regions. Modernity at large saw light as a positive source of health, both physical and mental, whereas the artistic engagement with darkness is clearly a late-modern orientation.

NORDIC URBANITY

Although Nordic urban forms throughout the ages have reflected European models, Nordic settlements, towns, and cities have their distinct characteristics and identities, from the clusters of miniaturized houses in the Faroe Islands to the medieval Swedish townscapes, Norwegian fishing towns, and the neoclassical wooden towns of the eighteenth and nineteenth centuries in Finland. Like architecture, modern town planning in the North followed the ideas and ideals of its European contemporaries. But regardless of their fundamentally universal theoretical or formal ground, Nordic towns, residential areas, and garden suburbs possess their own identities and have been regarded as models of democratic planning. Many of the Swedish and Norwegian postwar residential areas as well as Finnish garden suburbs, such as Tapiola, west of Helsinki, simultaneously reflect the ideals of social integration and equality, and the desire to fuse nature and human settlement. (Fig. 6) Postwar housing areas,

Fig. 6 Tapiola Garden
City, Espoo, Finland, 1950s.
A model of the Nordic
garden and forest town.

especially in Finland, reveal a unique aspiration to merge topological forest space with geometric architectural space into residential settings that have often paradoxically been called "forest towns."

Although cold climate and winter conditions with snow and ice are characteristic of the North, deliberate attempts to create special Winter Cities are rare.[9] It is interesting to note that the most determined proponent for Winter Cities was Erskine—who was not a native northerner—in his schemes for subarctic cities, such as An Ecological Arctic Town (1958), a dense conglomerate of buildings located on the southern slope of a mountain and protected from cold northern winds by a surrounding wall-like building. These ideas were developed further in his project "74°43' latitude north, 34°59' latitude west" for Resolute Bay, in the Northwest Territories of Canada. He also developed an interesting prefabricated house scheme for the project, with an aerodynamic shape to reduce heat loss. The Danish Henning Larsen's buildings for the University of Trondheim (1970, 1974–78) in Norway are an example of the attempt to create a continuous, covered, and climatically controlled pedestrian area. A similar glass-enclosed and covered town center was projected for the center of Tapiola in 1968 by a group of Finnish architects, but the scheme was not executed.[10] The Winter Cities Association has since 1983 promoted the development of city structures, as well as planning and design principles suited for cold climates. Climatically controlled urban units have more recently been created in several of the Nordic cities in various renewal projects for city centers as well as large office and shopping complexes, as in Stockholm and Oslo.

THE THREAT OF CONSUMERISM

In the entire consumer world today, architecture as an authentic art form is threatened. As architecture loses its artistic autonomy and existential sincerity, it is in danger of becoming mere utility, commodity, merchandise, and spectacle. This tendency is clearly visible also in the Nordic countries. A shallow corporate architecture or routine pragmatism, reduced to mere visual imagery, has often replaced architecture that is rooted in place, tradition, and fundamental existential experiences. A weakening of the sense of tradition is apparent in the rapid expansion of the universal architectural kitsch of consumerism that reflects both the loss of a sense of authentic tradition and the dramatically expanded mobility of people, products, styles, and ideas.

The unification of Europe has been regarded by its opponents as a threat to national identities and local cultures. The power of cultures to maintain their characteristics is, however, amazing, and the entire history of architecture proves that interaction hardly poses a threat to the identity of culture. On the contrary, a dynamic development of cultures arises from interaction. But the domination of materialism and the elimination of the spiritual dimensions of life altogether represent a form of cultural erosion from within, one that can have disastrous consequences even in the most determined stronghold of the modern tradition. This situation makes the architect's duty clear: our task is to defend the autonomy and authenticity of culture and human existential experience.

The Northern Dimension: Between Universality and Locality

A RETURN TO CULTURE-SPECIFIC ARCHITECTURE

A rationalist, constructive, and minimalist line has coexisted with the regionalist orientation in Nordic architectural thinking since the beginning of the twentieth century. This reflects the hidden moral code of a culture of scarcity deriving essentially from immemorial peasant conditions.

Since the 1980s the homogenization of culture and the consequent loss of the sense of local specificity in modern culture and architecture have increasingly been discussed by writers and designers. Today there seems to be a shift back to culture-specific and mythopoetic dimensions of architecture, bringing with it a renewed interest in the power of landscape and place, including a continued retension and interest in the Nordic vernacular.

The unavoidable shift toward sustainability, and the consequent interest in phenomena of nature and ecological principles, will certainly help to reroot architecture in its local soil. Instead of eliminating the special demands created by the climate, northern architecture is destined to use these conditions again as inspiration for essential architectural motifs. The recent, somewhat romantic ice architecture—such as ice hotels, bars, and chapels—and international exhibitions of artistic ice structures also indicate an interest in the exotic dimensions of the North. On the other hand, technology and new materials already permit architecture that reacts to the changes of seasons and weather in the ways that all life-forms in nature adapt to the ever-changing conditions of survival.

1   The concepts "North" and "northern" are vaguely defined notions of geography as well as cultural and political language. This essay discusses various aspects of dwelling and architecture roughly above 60° northern latitude: from Iceland in the west to the eastern border of Finland. In this framing of the subject, the considerable cold of winter and snow cover are essential aspects of living conditions.

The familiar term "Nordic countries" includes the Scandinavian countries proper (Sweden, Norway, and Denmark), and Finland and Iceland. Due to the focus on climatically northern architecture, Danish architecture has been excluded.

In his book *Nightlands: Nordic Building* (Cambridge, MA, and London: MIT Press, 1996), Christian Norberg-Schulz uses the notion "Nightlands" as a synonym for *north, mezzanotte* (midnight, in Italian) in reference to the Nordic countries.

2   See, for instance, Edward T. Hall, *The Hidden Dimension* (New York: Doubleday, 1969); Hall, *Beyond Culture* (New York: Doubleday, 1976).

3   Mildred Reed Hall and Edward T. Hall, *The Fourth Dimension in Architecture: The Impact of Building On Behaviour* (Santa Fe, NM: Sunstone Press, 1975), 8.

4   See Amos Rapoport, *House Form and Culture* (Englewood Cliffs, NJ: Prentice-Hall, Inc., 1969).

5   Göran Schildt, *Alvar Aalto: The Early Years* (New York: Rizzoli, 1984), 168, 254.

6   See, for instance, Sigfried Giedion, *Space, Time and Architecture: The Growth of a New Tradition* (Cambridge, MA: Harvard University Press, 1949).

7   See Juhani Pallasmaa, "Image and Meaning," in *Alvar Aalto: Villa Mairea 1938–39*, ed. Juhani Pallasmaa (Helsinki: Alvar Aalto Foundation and Mairea Foundation, 1998), 70–103.

8   To my knowledge, the first explicit study of light in Finnish architecture was Leonardo Mosso's essay "La luce nell'architettura di Alvar Aalto," *Estratto da Zodiac* 7 (1960).

9   Winter Cities is a concept for communities in northern latitudes that encourages them to plan their transportation systems, buildings, and recreation projects around the idea of using their infrastructure during all four seasons, rather than just two seasons (summer and autumn).

10   Erkki Juutilainen, Erkki Kairamo, Kirmo Mikkola, and Juhani Pallasmaa, Tapiola Center Plan, 1966–69.

Juhani Pallasmaa

CANADIAN ARCHITECTURE AND THE NORTH

Lisa Rochon

Since the 1940s a uniquely Canadian architecture has developed across the land, rooted in the values of human scale, material warmth, and deep connections to site. This body of work resides in cities and beyond, in the countryside, and in the wilds of the hinterland. It is elegant and livable—it resonates with the humanity of this country.

Ways of creating intelligent, enduring architecture have been passed down through the generations to contemporary Canadian designers. Wood is handled with special reverence: mammoth timbers are treated with the honesty of the northwest aboriginal building traditions, with thinner members of Douglas fir or cedar to suit a more fragile, urban scale. Light is welcomed as an essential, life-sustaining element. In Canada, architecture grows out of the landscape. And the Canadian landscape is mythic, Herculean in its scale and power. It is omnipresent and noble, given to moments of tenderness and terrible rages. Up north, architecture digs into the side of a hill or a mountain. Or it rises up to match the temper of the land. The late Arthur Erickson, who died in 2009, delivered architecture that honored and amazed. His poured-in-place concrete buildings were symphonies of unfliching cadence and passion for the land, work such as Simon Fraser University (1965) in Burnaby, British Columbia, and the Museum of Anthropology (1976) in Vancouver. Through his temples of civic architecture, he asked Canadians to dream big. He rightly deserves to be called Canada's greatest modern architect.

From the earliest history in Canada, people have created shelter directly from the land. With the igloo, the pit house, and the soddy, the site provided immediate and accessible architecture. Now, contemporary practitioners in Canada are reaching back to site and, like their ancestors, looking there for clues and triggers to guide their architecture. (Fig. 1)

Some like to mythologize Canada as a place of igloos and tepees. In truth, those structures represent the ultimate in land architecture. A large snow house or igloo would typically feature a sequence of domed passages—cold traps—that were scooped out of the ground. The main shelter was a vaulted dome constructed from blocks of snow inclined a little more with each layer. Such was the ingenious design of the igloo, accomplished without scaffold or external support, and appearing like balloons on the Arctic landscape.

In Canada, there is an unabashed intimacy between architecture and the landscape. Pit houses discovered in the interior of British Columbia, in the Nicola Valley, were first constructed some five thousand years ago. The structure began as a large hole in the ground, over which a circular roof of logs was built. Cedar bark and excavated earth were layered over the concentric rafters and packed down hard to keep out heavy rainfall. A ladder would be inserted through the smoke hole to allow for its inhabitants—sometimes up to thirty people—to climb in and out.

There was a time when European settlers new to Canada used the land to build what they could and survive. The soddy was a rough structure whose walls were constructed of long strips of thick sod, stacked green side down and laid in double rows. In the twenty-first century, Canada's important architecture is constructed of concrete, wood, and perhaps rusted steel, but the principle of extruding a shape from the land still holds today.

The Vancouver architect Peter Cardew "took the ground up and over" for the school that he designed for the Stone Indian Band in the Chilcotin region of interior British Columbia. It was a way of creating an affiliation with the landscape and communicating with the elders, many of whom did not speak English. In the tradition of the pit house, the school is partly submerged underground and partly articulated as a rough-hewn lean-to. The Montreal architect Gilles Saucier, who represented Canada at the Venice Biennale in 2004, finds resonance in the Kamouraska region of eastern Quebec where he grew up—the rocky outcrops like moments of violence dropped down on the slow unfolding of the St. Lawrence floodplain. The idea of rock cutting a jagged profile on the landscape is echoed in Saucier + Perrotte Architects' startling design for the Collège Gérald-Godin in Sainte Geneviève outside of Montreal. At the Perimeter Institute for Theoretical Physics in Waterloo, Ontario, the architects created a topographical fiction of grass berms and water, a theatrical landscape into which they inserted a powerful building.

Fig. 1 Replicas of Norse sod houses stand at the site of a thousand-year-old settlement at L'Anse Aux Meadows National Historic Park on the northern tip of Newfoundland, Canada.

The authenticity of the work of Brian MacKay-Lyons derives in part from its honest, stripped-down minimalism, which borrows from the cedar-shake barns and sheds of Nova Scotia's South Shore. Overhangs are eliminated to prevent shakes from being ripped off in the fierce winds coming off the Atlantic. MacKay-Lyons also takes cues from the design of traditional buildings. (Fig. 2)

Canada's first modernists started producing architecture that rubbed shoulders with the landscape. Ron Thom and Erickson were Vancouver boys, mountain climbers and canoeists who came to architecture through art, prodded into their wakeful state by artists such as Lawren Harris, Jack Shadbolt, and Bert Binning. While modernism was something they understood not merely as an architectural proposition but as a reflection of society's new beliefs, they were uniquely interested in how to connect architecture to the landscape. To them, that mattered much more than purely functional design. Perhaps the vast distance and isolation from the world's cultural centers empowered them. Or the brooding splendor of the mountains that surrounded them. Thom, Erickson, and many of their colleagues in Vancouver allowed themselves to romance the object, creating architecture that fell in love with the land around it.

Fig. 2 Brian MacKay-Lyons, Rubadoux Studio, Nova Scotia, Canada, 1990

Pierre Thibault's architectural work is designed with sensitive siting and crisp, contemporary lines. But it is his land art that testifies to his profound connection to the North. Over the last several years, Lac Turgeon has become his muse. It belongs to a chain of small lakes located in the ethereal landscape of the taiga in the Parc des Grands-Jardins, a provincial park in Quebec. The landscape is defined by forests of black spruce so fragile and thin that they look as if they have been burned. Here Thibault constructs with ice, snow, light, and fire—at once cutting a mile-long trench into a frozen lake and lighting it with a thousand candles. Thibault's work is part of an important body of Canadian architecture deeply aligned with the land. This interest in the significance and uniqueness of site, whether in rural Canada or the country's big cities, draws on the legacy handed down by Thom and Erickson. (Fig. 3)

Fig. 3 Pierre Thibault, *Les Jardins d'Hiver*, Lac Turgeon, Quebec, Canada, 2001

Pierre Thibault

Fig. 4 Shim-Sutcliffe
Architects, Moorelands
Camp Dining Hall, Dorset,
Ontario, Canada, 2001

Fig. 5 Patkau Architects,
Seabird Island School,
Agassiz, British Columbia,
Canada, 1991

The Toronto architects and partners Brigitte Shim and Howard Sutcliffe (of Shim-Sutcliffe Architects) use their work to create and manipulate the landscape. In their latest work, including the audacious integral house with its wooden ceilings and curving curtain wall that undulates five stories above a Toronto ravine, the architects pay their respects to the finely tuned works of the Finnish master, Aalto. But Shim came to understand site profoundly while working as a junior architect for Erickson on the West Coast. Sutcliffe also worked for Thom after he left Vancouver for Toronto to expand his award-winning practice. The legacy of the Vancouver modernists lives on in Shim-Sutcliffe's practice. (Fig. 4, see also pages 206–11)

ONE OF THE MOST famous examples of Canadian architecture that resonates with both the land and identity is Seabird Island School (1991) designed by Patkau Architects of Vancouver. (Fig. 5) Its strong, zoomorphic massing mirrors the surrounding coastal range of mountains on the delta near Agassiz, British Columbia, approximately seventy-five miles east of Vancouver. It can be understood as a piece of expressionist sculpture in a very large room. Heavy timber post and beam construction—the traditional building technique of the Pacific Northwest Indians—was modernized to use paralaminated columns and beams with steel connections on a reinforced-concrete-grade beam-and-pile foundation. Unskilled band members, who relied on a detailed framing model supplied by the architects to supplement conventional construction documents, erected much of the structure. The Patkau Architects' language of architecture is rooted in activism and prompts a heightened attention to the site.

For the aboriginal people of Canada, culture and place are inseparable. Architecture that still represented old models of repression needed to be abandoned and even demolished. More than twenty aboriginal schools, many of them recipients of national architecture awards, have been designed and constructed since 1985 in remote areas of British Columbia. The ongoing portfolio of important architecture work is due in large part to Marie-Odile Marceau, who spearheaded the initiative as architect in charge of British Columbia for the federal Ministry of Indian and Northern Affairs. Marceau actively engaged the First Nations communities in school vision planning and paired them with Vancouver architects acclaimed for their regional sensitivities and innovative forms. Most, like Seabird Island School, the T'lisalagi'lakw Elementary School by Henry Hawthorn Architect Ltd. (1994) for the Nimpkish Band in Alert Bay, and Chief Matthews Primary School (1993) at Old Massett, Haida Gwaii (Queen Charlotte Islands) by Acton Ostry Architects, are loved by their communities. Not all of the tribes, however, have taken on cultural ownership of the new schools. (Fig. 6)

An image of civic gathering is strongly expressed with Busby+Associates Architects' Nicola Valley Institute of Technology (2002) in Merritt, British Columbia. Shared by both aboriginal and nonaboriginal communities, the institute was designed as a cold-climate energy-efficient building, drawing on Busby's acclaimed expertise in green building design. The structure emanates from the sloping site and grows into a three-story edifice, creating a strong figure in the forested landscape. The "inner strip" of the semicircular rooftop is planted, adding to the sense of the emergence from the landscape. About four hundred students attend the University College of the Cariboo and the Nicola Valley Institute of Technology; instruction is available on campus in the five languages still spoken by aboriginal persons in the Okanagan Valley of British Columbia.

Early in their practice, Shim-Sutcliffe Architects engaged with the landscape of the North, designing a house in Ontario's Beaver Valley surrounded by an apple orchard (1989), another on a pastoral island in the St. Lawrence River (1990), and a boathouse in Muskoka (2000), the province's popular mecca for cottages. The Moorelands Camp Dining Hall (2002) (see also pages 206–11), located south of Algonquin Park near Dorset, Ontario, at a summer camp for inner-city kids, sits on a knoll overlooking Kawagama Lake, the largest body of water in Lake of Bays, with about one thousand cottages surrounding it. In form, Moorelands mimics the rough aluminum barns located along Highway 35. What animates these traditional structures are the skylights that run along the length of their roofs. The Moorelands Camp Dining Hall is similarly lit by a skylight; it is, in fact, a motorized greenhouse glazing system that can be opened or closed with the push of a button. For the dining hall, the architects specified a deceptively simple structure of glue-lam trusses combined with small-scale narrow lumber.

Fig. 6 Acton Ostry Architects, Chief Matthews Primary School, Old Massett, Haida Gwaii, British Columbia, Canada, 1993.

TODAY MORE THAN 80 percent of Canadians are urbanized, living in large metropolitan areas with increasingly strong urban architecture by Canadian architects based in Vancouver, Toronto, and Montreal. The inspired redevelopment of Woodward's department store by Henriquez Partners into a mixed-use, mixed-income community is a critical step toward healing Vancouver's troubled downtown Eastside. The new Manitoba Hydro Headquarters (2009) in Winnipeg by Kuwabara Payne McKenna Blumberg Architects (KPMB) is a work of deep sustainability and urban place making. The cultural rebranding of Toronto has produced seven new monuments by local talents and world stars. Frank Gehry returned to his hometown to reinvent the art gallery of Ontario (2008) with sumptuous wood-lined promenades, interior courtyards, and serpentine stairs clad in Douglas fir. Despite the economic recession of 2009, public commissions—university buildings, public libraries, hospitals, aquatic centers, schools, and cultural centers—have helped to temper the slowdown in the commercial sector. Firms such as Moriyama & Teshima architects, Diamond+Schmitt architects, and Hariri Pontarini Architects are helping to export the Canadian sensibilities around the world.

But still, ways of dwelling lightly on the land preoccupy Canadians. Just as the nomadic Mi'kmaq on the East Coast constructed wigwams of spruce poles and sheets of birch bark that could be erected in a day and dismantled easily enough, the tiles of bark saved for the next camp, light structures still continue to dot the Canadian landscape, and the cottage and cabin—sublimely sited and beautifully detailed—are significant building types in Canada. While concrete-and-steel structures make up the impressive architecture of the cities, in suburban and rural Canada, designers demonstrate a continued interest in a slowed-down, enduring kind of architecture.

The Group of Seven artist Lawren Harris, who favored northern sites for painting, asserted that cleansing spiritual energy flowed from the North. It is no myth that Canadians are attracted to the North, whether for its own mystical appeal or merely from the need to escape the city. North is that large expanse in an atlas, which extends beyond the United States. That map indicates a territory that is vast and full of potential. North is simply a point of departure.

Excerpted from *Up North: Where Canada's Architecture Meets the Land* (Toronto: Key Porter Books Limited, 2005).

Canadian Architecture and the North

PROJECTS

THE NEW WING OF THE ANCHORAGE MUSEUM AT RASMUSON CENTER

project

architect **David Chipperfield Architects**
location / year Anchorage, Alaska / 2009

The glass facade reflects the urban surroundings and the sky.

The ambitious 80,000-square-foot expansion of the Anchorage Museum at Rasmuson Center by architect David Chipperfield responded to the shortcomings of the existing building, which was built in the era of museums that did not have views in or out, and which had a main entrance that faced away from the heart of the rest of the downtown. His design provided a new main entrance facing west and a unique facade composed of insulated fritted glass striped with mirrored glass that reflects the sky and surrounding mountains. The constantly changing surface "takes on the light qualities that are here," said Chipperfield. "One of the great materials of Alaska is the light."

The glazing and pattern were designed specifically to meet the challenges of the extreme environment: allowing natural light in while minimizing the glare from the low angle of the northern sun, and resisting condensation that comes with temperature swings and precipitation. The glass panels were preassembled prior to shipping for easy installation and, as the skin of the new addition, contrast overtly with the original building's brick-clad exterior.

A public plaza links the museum with the downtown area through a birch-tree forest planted inside a two-acre sanctuary that offers open-air spaces for nature exploration, quiet reflection, outdoor activities, and a permanent sculpture, *Habitat*, by British artist Antony Gormley.

The more than six hundred four-foot-wide glass panels that make up the facade allow an interchange between the outside and inside. Transparent sections of glass allow views inside the building, while transluscent sections allow for reflection. Natural light enhances the experience of the visitor when traveling through the building's interior, preventing the "museum fatigue" that can come from closed-in, darkened spaces. This use of light deliberately contrasts with antiquated notions of museums as dark boxes with the sole purpose of protecting the objects inside. Chipperfield took advantage of new technologies in UV protection—which allow for transparency without compromising protection from ultraviolet rays—to incorporate natural light, which in turn influences individual interior spaces made distinct through different colors and materials.

At the same time, the four-story building promises dramatic views that drive gallery organization and traffic flow. The flow is vertical: visitors head to temporary exhibits by climbing a large metal staircase that adds a sculptural element to the interior. Third-floor galleries feature a view of downtown Anchorage and the Alaska Range, while the fourth-floor gallery offers a unique reward—an expansive view of the Chugach Foothills as a backdrop to the city.

To contrast with the cool temperatures outside, Chipperfield used a palette of warm colors and natural materials in the interior to provide a sense of welcome as visitors enter the building. The first-floor public spaces differ starkly from the neutrality of the glass and the cool blue of the sky and surrounding mountains. The entry lobby features bright yellow metal panels between concrete columns, to form walls, and a bright yellow fiberglass front desk. The cafe, just off the main entrance, is deep red, and the towering walls surrounding the main staircase are clad with wood panels. The exhibition galleries return the building to a subtle palette, with charcoal gray floors of poured concrete and the repeating forms of concrete columns.

The glass panels allow an interchange between the outside and inside.

The New Wing of the Anchorage Museum at Rasmuson Center

1 The museum's glass facade provides a constantly changing surface.

2 View of original structure beyond the new glass counterpart

3 The building sits between the mountains and the sea.

4 Second-floor, east-facing facade, with reflection of existing museum structure

5 The Anchorage Museum faces west toward a new public plaza designed by Charles Anderson Landscape Architects and Anchorage's downtown core.

The New Wing of the Anchorage Museum at Rasmuson Center

6 The fourth-floor gallery
provides views toward the
mountains to the east.

7 Museum cafe

8 Main stair in lobby

David Chipperfield

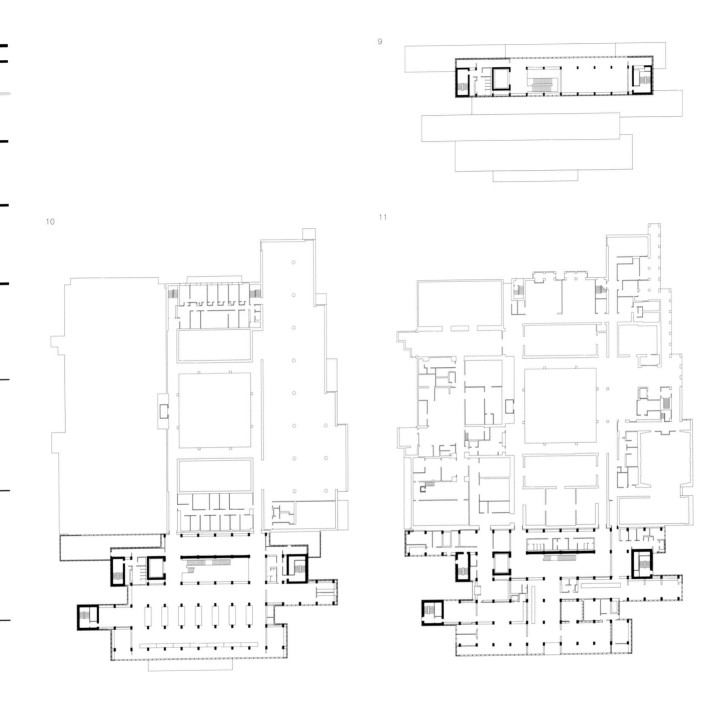

The New Wing of the Anchorage Museum at Rasmuson Center

12

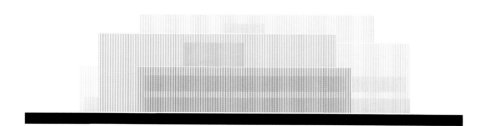

9 Fourth-floor plan, with
gallery space that offers
views out to the Chugach
Mountain range

10 Second-floor plan,
housing the objects on
long-term loan from the
Smithsonian Museum
of Natural History and
the National Museum of
the American Indian as
part of the Arctic Studies
Center

11 First-floor plan,
housing public areas
such as the lobby,
resource center, shop,
and cafe

12 from top to bottom
South elevation
North elevation
West elevation

13 clockwise from top left
West section
East section
South section

13

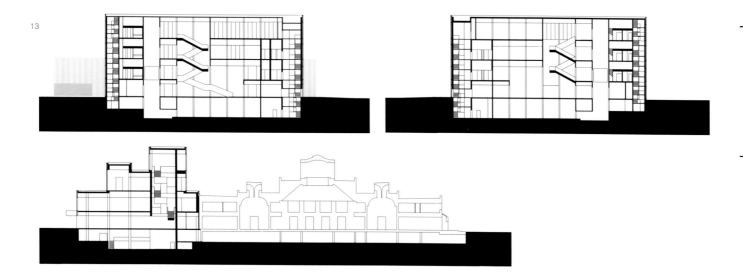

David Chipperfield

49

59°N
JAN. 27°F
mean
temperatures **JULY 61°F**

KARMØY FISHING MUSEUM

project

architect **Snøhetta**
location / year Karmøy, Norway / 1998

The museum is poised on the precipice of a small cliff on the west cost of Norway.

Poised on the precipice of a small cliff on the west cost of Norway, the Karmøy Fishing Museum is an institution dedicated to the seafaring and fishing culture of the region. With load-bearing in-situ concrete walls that allow the structure to cantilever twenty-three feet over the surrounding terrain, the 4,320-square-foot building establishes a sculptural presence over the surrounding houses and buildings, many of which were once used in the fishing industry.

Due to the decline of the village's main source of income, beginning in the 1980s with a variety of impacts on the fishing industry such as overfishing, Snøhetta developed the building's design on a low budget, intentionally contrasting it with the houses constructed of wood nearby through the use of industrial materials such as steel, concrete, and glass. The building has presence but is not overly imposing.

One of the large side windows is flanked by a framed wall clad with traditionally woven screens made from native coastal bushes and can be easily removed and extended later on. The interior also allows great flexibility so that exhibits can be arranged in multiple ways and on several levels.

Though simple in many ways, the long, thin proportions of the building distinguish it from other structures by creating a giant window to the sea. Stretching about 150 feet long, twenty-five feet wide, the museum sits perpendicular to the ocean as if a lens stretching from land to water. The green-hued floor is finished with epoxy, and side windows reveal sheep meadows at either side. The sixteen-square-foot concrete panels that make up the facade were treated with a fertilizing chemical that allows moss to grow on the outside, much like the fungi, moss, and grass that grows on coastal rocks and boulders nearby.

A concrete facade contrasts with the natural surroundings.

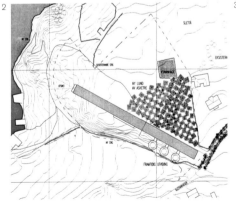

Karmøy Fishing Museum

4

1 Concrete facade of the building as it extends toward the sea

2 Site plan

3 The setting is a picturesque fjord surrounded by small, white houses and sheds, many of which were, at one time, connected to the fishing industry.

4 Wood, metal, and concrete provide the interior materials, with large glass windows offering views beyond.

ORDISH ANDERSON RESIDENCE

project

architect **Kobayashi + Zedda Architects**
location / year Whitehorse, Yukon, Canada / 2003

Overhangs prevent allow for runoff of rain and snow and prevent snow buildup against the house.

Kobayashi + Zedda Architects designed this single-family residence for a Tlingit (native people of the northwestern Canada and southeast Alaska) artist and carver and his partner in Whitehorse, Yukon. The program outlined a setting for a creative work environment and simple living space.

Occupying a previously cleared portion of a rural site, the house nestles into its northern edge, making it able to comfortably absorb the low angle of winter sunlight and protecting it from winter exposure.

The building form follows the interior organization of active and passive spaces along a glazed east-west edge. Horizontally, the main entry simultaneously separates and connects the living areas from the areas of rest and bathing. The living areas are organized vertically, with a studio loft placed over the spaces for food preparation, dining, and living. Windows exposing a northern view of the adjacent boreal forest provide daylight and an intimate artist-studio space (for carving).

The southern wall of glass offers exposure to the changing light and color, as the most intense sun exposure comes from the south in northern communities. Looking back to the south facade of the house, the screen of spruce sticks imitates a boreal forest edge.

The design makes use of the unnecessarily large clearing left by the former owner: the home primarily occupies just the northern edge of the property and thereby allows the remainder of the site to recover. Stockpiled organic material is spread over the site to help encourage growth. Direct vehicle access to the house is discouraged in favor of a pedestrian path. The site provides a protective environment of mature spruce, pine, and willow. Long hours of summer sunlight are mitigated by a horizontal cedar-wood sunscreen, which lets in warmth and light but minimizes glare and provides some shelter. Rain and snow runoff from the roof is collected in recessed ground-level containers, to be used for the garden wand flowerbeds.

The house is primarily clad in Hardi-plank/cedar composite siding, which is lower in maintenance requirements than natural wood. Corrugated galvanized siding is used elsewhere on the facade for detail and contrast.

Spruce, pine, and willow trees populate the site.

55

Ordish Anderson Residence

4

1 The house is primarily clad in Hardi-plank/cedar composite siding, strapping, and a south-facing screen.

2 South facade spruce-wood screen over windows

3 Spruce-wood screen on south facade inter-sects with metal siding

4 View of living room with south-facing windows

5

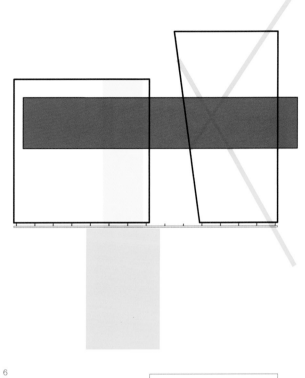

6

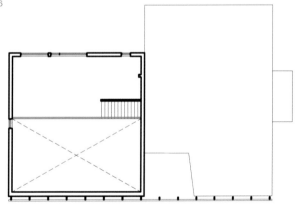

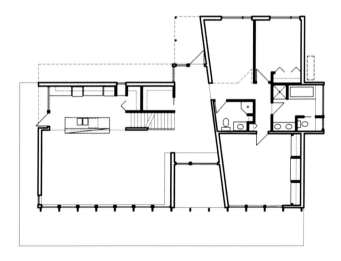

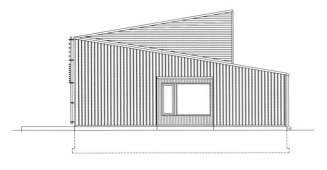

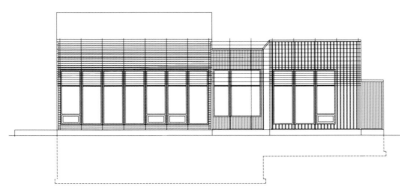

5 Daylight studies helped guide the window place-ment and the wood slats to mitigate the harsh light created by the low angle of the sun while maximiz-ing natural light.

6 left and right
Second-floor plan
First-floor plan

7 top and bottom
East elevation
South elevation

8 Sections

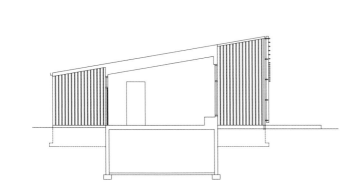

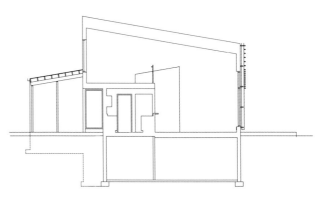

Kobayashi + Zedda Architects

MONASTERY FOR CISTERCIAN NUNS

project

architect **Jensen & Skodvin**
location / year Tautra Island, Norway / 2006

One of four main rooms that also serve as corridors or circulation areas.

The monastery resides on Tautra Island in the Trondheimsfjord region of Norway and serves as a convent for eighteen nuns from many countries, predominately the United States, and all of the Cistercian order. The introverted character of the nuns' daily life prompted Jensen & Skodvin to develop an environment of privacy and exclusion through a low building with a series of gardens. The design brings in light and opens up spectacular views from the refectories and dining hall, where the nuns sit at one side of the table and look silently through the glass wall, to the fjord and mountains on the other side.

The first Cistercian monastery in Norway was established on Tautra Island eight hundred years ago on a site surrounded by coastline and farmland. The site remains appropriately quiet and appealing for the new monastery. The 21,528-square-foot building consists of a horizontal layout with a church, library, kitchen, cloister, chapter room, scriptorium, reflectorium (a quiet, meditative space), and an area for crafts and other activities, along with guest rooms, offices, and sleeping/private quarters.

Glass, stone, and wood are used as primary materials, which gives the building variation in texture and hue. Laminated spruce wood is used for interior wall construction, with pillars placed where the laminated sheets come together. On the exterior, thin stripes of differently colored slate stones from a local quarry are fastened to the building with metal clamps. The stones blend harmoniously with the nearby rocky shoreline of the island and the surrounding grassy meadows but offer a geometry to the building in their square-tile application. The plan reduced the original layout for the preexisting monastery by 30 percent and eliminated corridors altogether by taking into account how the monestary works. Typically, the nuns assemble together in one of the four main rooms, which can also serve as corridors or circulation areas. These rooms connect with one another at the corners, with courtyards between them, creating seven garden areas that increase the intersection of natural light and create a more communal feeling for the daily life of the nuns.

Except for the cells, each space has a distinct identity. The nuns participated in the design process, providing insight into their routines, rituals, and needs, and they helped plan the landscaping and fencing in the gardens and convent with the guidance and labor of landscaping and construction professionals from the local congregation.

Stone facade with metal roofing, horizontal windows, and wood doors, detail

New Monastery for Cistercian Nuns

The facade is covered in differently colored stones fastened to the building with metal clamps.

Jensen & Skodvin

New Monastery for Cistercian Nuns

1 Aerial view shows the placement of the monastery within the scenic landscape

2 Lateral view of facade, with view out over Tautra island and the Trondheimsfjord

3 The garden area in winter

4 The building form creates distinct exterior spaces.

5 Slender horizontal windows offer views out and in, with the interior structure of the building visible from the outside.

New Monastery for Cistercian Nuns

6 Interior circulation corridor, with spectacular views of the fjord and mountains

7 Interior corridor of glass, stone, and wood

8 One of four main rooms that also serve as corridors or circulation areas

9 Refectory and dining hall windows face the landscape.

10 Looking up from inside the reflectorium

latitude **60°N**
JAN. 23°F
mean
temperatures **JULY 60°F**

ST. HENRY'S ECUMENICAL ART CHAPEL

project

architect **Sanaksenaho Architects**
location / year Turku, Finland / 2005

Clad on the inside with wood and on the outside with copper, St. Henry's Ecumenical Art Chapel in Turku has a ceiling forty feet high at its peak. The patina on its exterior copper cladding, which gradually becomes green over time, blends with the pine trees and resembles the old village church. Likewise, sunlight will turn the smattering of untreated timber in the interior a reddish color.

The chapel stands upon a hillock of pine and spruce on the island of Hirvensalo, an area characterized by open fields and wooded hills. The shape of the building contours to the land. From the outside, the building looks like a fin, fish, or upturned boat with a weathered skin of rectangular scales. The form references the traditional architecture of churches of many denominations, including the various churches involved in supporting the chapel (Catholic, Lutheran, Orthodox), as well as in its function as a place of consolation and hope.

Inside, tapered ribs of laminated pine rise at six-foot intervals and provide a complex surface off of which light radiates as it enters through the altar window. Between the ribs, untreated pine boarding forms a curved lining. The narrow yet expansive form harkens back to the story of Jonah and the whale and the sense of traveling on a vast and unknowable sea. The building's nave is organized into two parts: the chapel up front and the gallery in back. Visitors can study works of art during the service and walk eastward toward the light by moving into the chapel space.

Waxed pine floorboard planks, just under eight inches wide and two inches thick, run the length of the space. Footsteps clack like they do in old churches. Vestry benches and hat racks made of solid alder with laminated edges provide simple furnishings in the mostly bare interior. The space fills itself, in a way, and opens up the possibility for those inside to reflect and connect in sacred ways.

The chapel currently ranks second in the number of people visiting Finnish religious sites. The original design included an altar by Finnish sculptor Kain Tapper, who died before completing his work. The chapel still does not have an altar.

St. Henry's Ecumenical Art Chapel

1 South facade upon
approach to chapel

2 South facade showing
window treatment
that allows light in
from the east

3 West facade and
chapel entrance

4 Skylight

5 Interior work space

St. Henry's Ecumenical Art Chapel

Sanaksenaho Architects

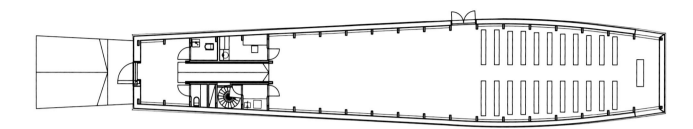

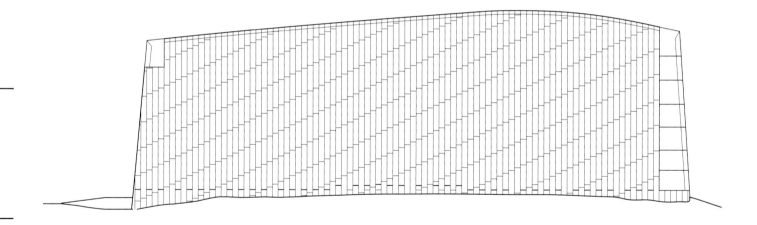

9

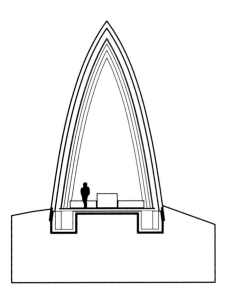

10

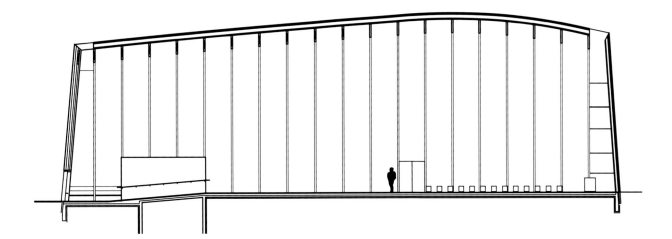

VILLA IN ARCHIPELAGO

project

architect **Tham & Videgård Hansson Architects**
location / year Stockholm, Sweden / 2006

Latticework creates light and shadow.

In the Villa in Archipelago a simple, but dramatic, intersection occurs between the woodlands of the island of Husaro in the archipelago of Stockholm and its inhabitants. The site is located on a flat area of mountainous region, in a wooded island of mature pines, and Tham & Videgård Hansson Architects oriented the horizontal building to take advantage of sunlight from the south and views of the Baltic Sea to the west.

The 1,400-square-foot summer home sits low in the landscape, with tall pines around it. Depending on the time of day and available sunlight, the house appears either concealed in shadows and trees or bathed in daylight. The building is lightweight construction in wood and glass on a simple platform frame; the black-stained fir plywood exterior references the wooded setting, and extensive glass surfacing reflects the water, often providing a mirror to the site.

The traditional steel framing and masonry, with massive woodwork inside and out, combine to give a hand-constructed feeling to the structure. The interior consists of light-hued materials and furnishings that contrast softly with the exterior. Floor-to-ceiling windows and sliding glass doors in the front rooms open up to vistas through the trees and to the sea a stone's throw away.

The small spaces, like the guest rooms and laundry, are in the back of the villa and larger social areas are in front in an open layout, divided only by sliding glass doors. The zigzag form of the interior guides movement and results in three interconnected decked terraces outside the master bedroom, living room, kitchen area, and studio, all with views of the sea. These outdoor spaces soak in the sunlight from above. Terrace floor planks of a light color mimic the earth around the house rather than the dark hue of the building's exterior.

1 West facade, which faces the Baltic Sea. The building is a lightweight construction in wood and glass on a simple platform frame.

2 West facade

Villa in Archipelago

The zigzag form creates three interconnected decked terraces outside the master bedroom, living room, kitchen area, and studio, all with views of the sea.

Tham & Videgård Hansson Architects

Villa in Archipelago

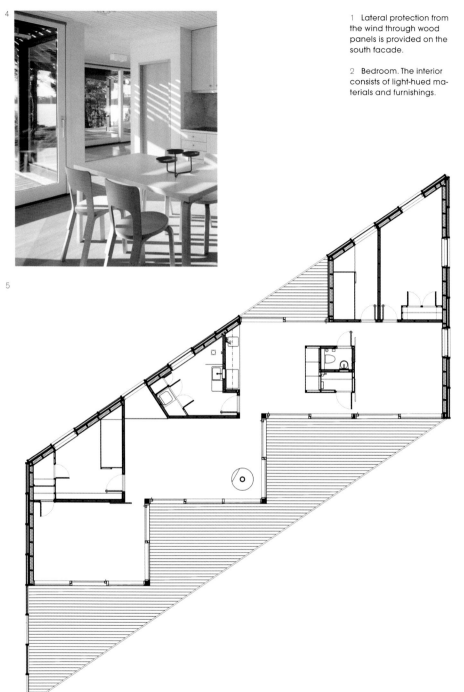

4

1 Lateral protection from the wind through wood panels is provided on the south facade.

2 Bedroom. The interior consists of light-hued materials and furnishings.

3 Living room

4 Kitchen. Natural light flows gently into all of the spaces within the house.

5 Plan, showing the open public spaces, zigzag pattern, and exterior decking that combine to create the overall form of the house

5

latitude **64°N**
JAN. 31°F
mean
temperatures **JULY 51°F**

project

SKRUDAS RESIDENCE

architect **Studio Granda**
location / year Reykjavik, Iceland / 2004

On the north side, the box twists slightly, punctuated by a series of flush openings that culminate in a corner window.

Iceland sits in the middle of the North Atlantic, just outside the Arctic Circle and on top of tectonic and volcanic activity—the country gets about an inch wider every year. Considering its high latitude, Iceland has a reasonably mild climate, but because of its unique geography, buildings are occasionally subject to significant volcanic eruptions and earthquakes. The landscape is almost entirely based on material of volcanic origin, including different types of lava, ash, dust, and rocks.

Reykjavik is spread across a peninsula with a panoramic view of the mountains and the Atlantic Ocean on almost all sides. Poised on the northern edge of Gardabær, one of Reykjavik's satellite towns, the Skrudas residence has an unbroken ocean view framed by Reykjavik's mountainous girdle. The tension between the closeness of suburban neighbors and the expanse of view inspired the design. Taking advantage of the setting, the Icelandic architecture firm Studio Granda emphasized multiple points of contact between the building and landscape.

In order to introduce a local sensibility and expertise, every element, including furniture and fixtures, of the 3,600-square-foot building was custom designed and produced locally in accordance with the plan hashed out among the architects and clients, who worked closely together throughout the process.

On the private garden side, to the south, the house includes a series of interconnected terraces with large sliding doors; the external form folds into itself to create a sheltered court around which the house wraps on three split levels. The main entry from the south brings people to the lower level, where they can access the garage and lower-level bedrooms, including an au-pair bedroom. This low-ceilinged entry opens up to a double-height limestone-clad family room with large sliding doors, which lead out into the garden. Upstairs, the kitchen, dining room, and living room afford panoramic views of the capital city and the Atlantic Ocean.

The interior finishes center on a simple palette of black walnut, limestone, and stainless steel in a series of white volumes that lighten the space. No dwelling spaces face the street and the only fenestration is the sandblasted glass of the garage doors, where privacy is not as important. To the north, the box twists slightly, punctuated by a series of flush openings that culminate in a corner window.

The structure consists of in-situ concrete, some of which is exposed to highlight the construction and materiality of the form, with a steel and timber roof. Clad entirely in flat-seamed copper, the house appears homogeneous.

North facade, with views
of the city beyond

Skrudas Residence

4

1 South facade facing courtyard

2 The top floor of the house offers views north and south.

3 Interior corridor with concrete, wood, and stone

4 The upstairs living room affords panoramic views of the capital region and Atlantic Ocean.

5 The low ceiling of the entry opens up to the double-height limestone-clad family room.

5

6

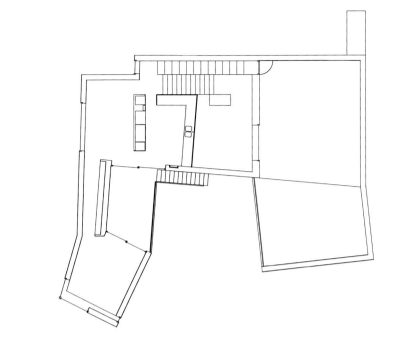

7

Skrudas Residence

8

9

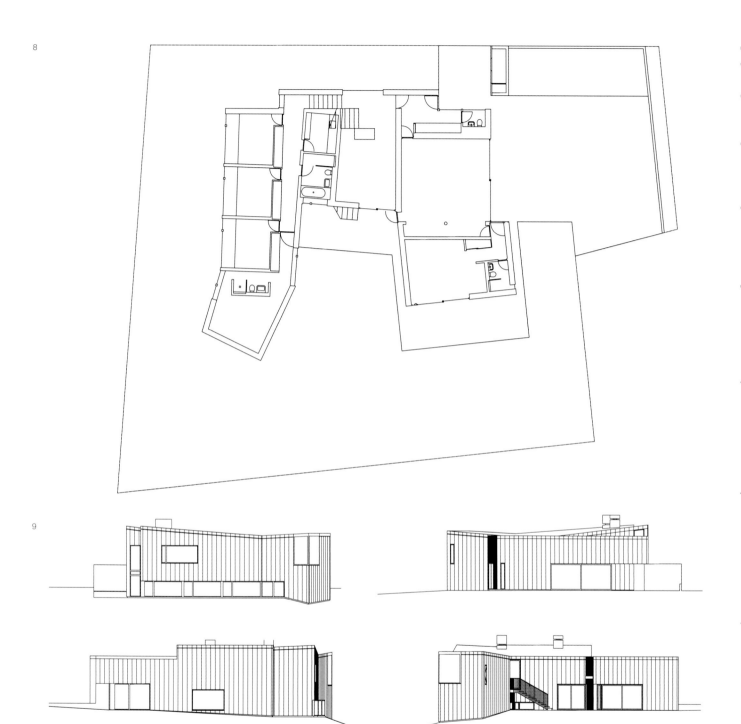

BUSER/ CHAPOTON RESIDENCE

project

architect **mayer sattler-smith**
location / year Big Lake, Alaska / 2009

Charred wood
facade, detail

The Buser/Chapoton residence sits on glacial marine sediment (a type of clay that occurs in high latitudes), tilted toward the Alaska Range. The 2,500-square-foot house sits on twenty acres and faces unoccupied land to the west, intensifying the sense of isolation and wilderness. Situated on the highest point of a hill, the house dominates an impressive panoramic sweep of mostly untouched landscape, with mountains rising at every horizon line.

The residence also overlooks the site of an old house that survived the devastating Miller's Reach fire in 1996. The owner of the house, dog musher Martin Buser, who won the Iditarod in 2002, saved his home from the flames of a large-scale forest fire that cut a swath of destruction across the valley and forced an areawide evacuation. Buser stayed at his home throughout the fire, dousing the land and the home with water. Still, Buser and his wife eventually desired a new home on higher ground that could take advantage of the views provided by the site. The existing home remains as a greeting house for visitors who come to see the sled dogs.

With simple materials of wood and concrete, mayer sattler-smith designed the new house—a wood-clad box with concrete forms. Blackened trees still dominate the area, and the exterior cladding of the house mimics the deep charcoal-black hue through the use of wood siding charred by the 1996 fire. Along the south side of the house, a twenty-four-foot outer stairway leads from the lower level to a roof terrace with a single fir tree. An outside reflecting pool does double-duty as a water tank for a sprinkler system.

Inside, the rooms orient toward the views, with north-facing windows that provide a view of the expansive setting. A fireplace that provides vertical bracing on the main floor flanks a floor-to-ceiling window that reveals the valley. From the rooftop deck, the vista is even more stunning and vast.

The architects did not design to a construction budget, since Buser did most of the actual building himself, trading sponsorship of his dog team for supplies and finding recycled materials or deals on his own. Instead, the architects designed a home that incorporates functional features and site-specific materials.

North facade with low
retaining wall

Buser/Chapoton Residence

4

1 View of home from the former house site to the north

2 A window is cut out of the charred wood facade.

3 View north of Alaska Range from main living area

4 View north from living room

5 Panoramic views from the roof deck

5

project

HOTEL KIRKENES

architect **Sami Rintala**
location / year Kirkenes Harbor, Finland / 2005

When asked by the city of Kirekenes, Finland, to build a piece of art in the small harbor town for the 2005 Barents Art Triennale, Sami Rintala opted for something useful—a simple hotel for hunters, sailors, backpackers, fortune-seekers, travelers, fishermen, and other travelers passing through the quaint town of six thousand residents. Though neither a cultural hub nor political center, the city sits in a region of northeast Norway on the Barents Sea where many cultures intersect, including Sámi, Russian, Norwegian, and Finnish. The economy tends to shift seasonally with an emphasis on industries like fishing, construction, and tourism.

The design embraces simplicity. Twenty feet long, sixteen feet high, and eight feet wide, the building looks stark and industrial from a distance, small and comfortable up close. The completely wooden structure stands on a lightweight foundation of concrete bricks and is anchored to pier rocks for stability. Its painted black exterior absorbs warmth from the sun to combat the cold sea air and increase efficiency, and it matches the color of the rocky seashore. On the outside wall facing north and the city, a giant

painted letter *H* identifies the hotel from the warehouses and containers nearby.

The 237-square-foot lodge contains one single room, one double room, and a small lobby. A single stove heats the entire building; guests go to the police station next door to use the bathroom and shower. The local tourist information office functions as the reception desk for the hotel. The interior is painted natural white for maximum light. It offers warmth, shelter, and views to the Barents Sea so that guests feel connected to the setting.

With a tight budget and a construction period of only ten days, a small team of builders, which included the architect and three architecture students, finished the hotel just three minutes before it opened. The same sense of urgency and ruggedness stays with the building to this day.

South facade facing the approach. The *H* on the west facade greets visitors and distinguishes the hotel from the warehouses and containers nearby.

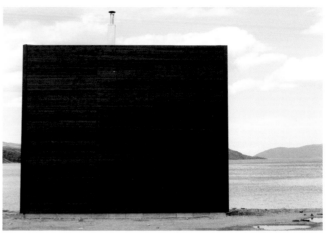

94   Hotel Kirkenes

1 View from hotel's interior

2 South facade

3 North facade facing the Barents Sea

4 Interior showing the ladder to one of the hotel's two bedrooms

5 The interior is painted natural white for maximum light and avoids unnecessary fineries and furnishings.

Sami Rintala

65°N
JAN. 39°F
JULY 57°F

project **PETTER DASS MUSEUM**

architect **Snøhetta**
location / year Alstahaug, Norway / 2007

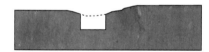

Concept diagram

Nestled between rock walls on a remote fjord in Norway, the Petter Dass Museum emerges from a man-made crevasse as if reaching beyond its rocky hold. The building's poetic elements suit its namesake, the Norwegian poet Petter Dass (1647–1707), priest of the nearby Alstahaug Church from 1689 to his death. He is one of the country's most important poets, and his writings reflect northern Norway's natural and human environment. Alstahaug has held a significant role as an ecclesiastical center in the Norwegian town of Helgeland since the thirteenth century; the historical importance of the site made the task of finding an appropriate spot for a new building challenging.

The shoreline farming region sits by the western slopes of the Seven Sisters mountain range. Norwegian firm Snøhetta's design positioned the freestanding building in a 230-foot-long, fifty-foot-wide gap chiseled out of a niche in the rocky ground. The placement melds the building with its landscape. An unpaved circular walkway leads to the building's entrance. Visitors can climb staircases and stroll on paths between the building's forms and the granite walls covered with moss. Window-filled walls on the building's ground floor further emphasize the relationship between the building and its natural surroundings. Glass surfaces at the ends of the elongated building present views of the church on one end and the sky on the other. At the upper floor, a zinc-sheathed, steel-framed form cantilevers twenty-three feet in front and back, angling in tandem with the ridge itself before rising above it.

The museum, with
windows into the lobby,
emerges from a man-
made crevasse.

Petter Dass Museum

Upper-floor cantilever,
covered in zinc

100   Petter Dass Museum

4

5

1 View from main entrance. The building is nestled between rock walls on a remote fjord.

2 View from exterior walkway to the church beyond

3 Windows at the end of the elongated building present landscape views.

4 Staircase running between two of the building's reflective surfaces

5 Longitudinal section, with Alstahang Church on the right

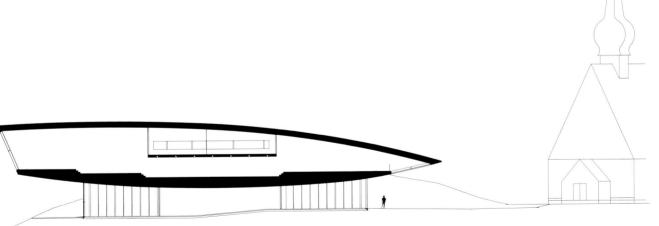

Snøhetta

project **VILLAGE SCHOOLS**

architect **Koonce Pfeffer Bettis Architects**
location / year **Akiak, Akiachak, and Tuluksak, Alaska / 2005**

The arctic fox is a resident of the Far North.

When designing three schools for the Yupiit School District and a fourth for the city of Kotlik in Alaska, Koonce Pfeffer Bettis had to consider the climate and logistical challenges of transporting supplies and materials to communities without road access. In these villages, where temperatures regularly reach -40°F, the river serves as the main conduit of life. People get around by planes, snowmobiles, and boats, and a mail plane arrives every day with supplies and goods. The fuel trucks, water trucks, and cranes required on a construction project arrive on barges and return the next year, as the construction season is restricted to the short summer season. Anything not anticipated for construction is flown in at great cost and delay.

Because low vegetation defines the landscape, large buildings are visible from one village to the next. Logistics may require thoughtful planning, and design considerations leave a lasting impression. Therefore, the design process includes many public meetings with community members and full-site planning.

The three schools in Akiak, Akiachuk, and Tuluksak take the basic form of a traditional native structure called the *qasgiq*,

or men's house, a communal building where men lived and the Yup'ik people held ceremonies, dances, rituals, and seasonal activities. An interpretation of the form, a wooden structure that forms a dome-like shape, dominates the entrance of the schools in the Yup'ik district, each school separated from the other by twenty miles, traversable by air or boat. They share the same basic plan with slightly different configurations, each housing eighty to 120 students and serving as a community hub and gathering place. The planning process for these projects included meetings with villagers, district officials, and elders.

The schools sit on steel piles with forty-eight- to sixty-inch water tables underneath them, which causes snow to blow under the buildings rather than forming drifts. Water tanks holding 10,000 to 15,000 gallons of water supply the sprinkler systems, and metal siding minimizes exterior maintenance. These are common construction methods in the North.

Though isolated, these schools provide sophisticated educational experiences via Wi-Fi connectivity and trail systems for outdoor activities. The larger communal areas are separated from classroom wings, which also allows the village residents to use the schools for community activities all year long. The abundance of natural light that enters the spaces and the use of bold colors and natural wood materials throughout the interior create a warm, welcoming atmosphere during every season.

Architectural elements, such as the arcs coming off the ends of the building, serve as snow fences to control drifting near entrances and windows. Materials used on the exterior, such as corrugated metal siding, were selected for their durability and low-maintenance requirements.

Architectural elements double as snow fences to control drifting near entrances and windows at Akiak.

1 Approach to
Akiak in winter

2 Simple and durable
building materials are
used at Akiak.

3 Interior circulation
area, Akiachak

4 Interior corridor at
Akiak, featuring bold
colors, natural wood
materials, and
natural light

5 Multipurpose room
featuring an interpreta-
tion of a traditional "men's
house" structure and
photographic murals with
portraits of native elders
by Kevin G. Smith.

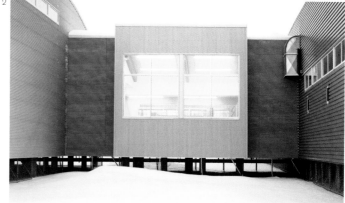

Koonce Pfeffer Bettis Architects

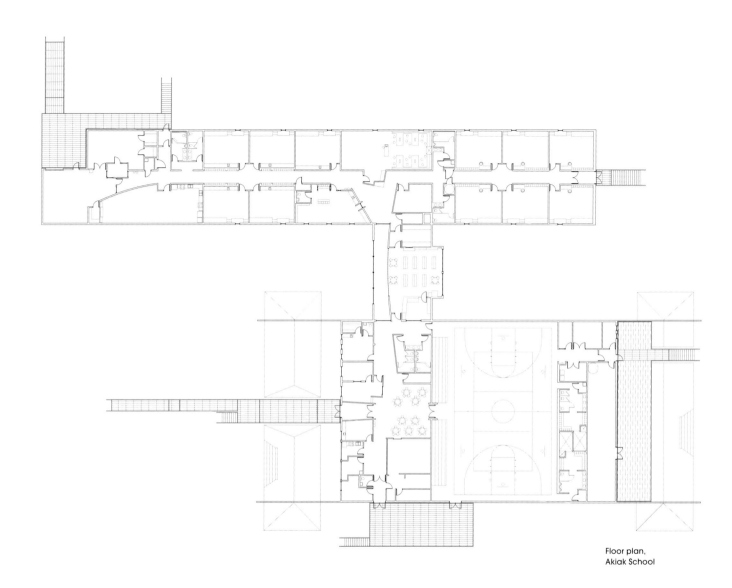

Floor plan,
Akiak School

Village Schools

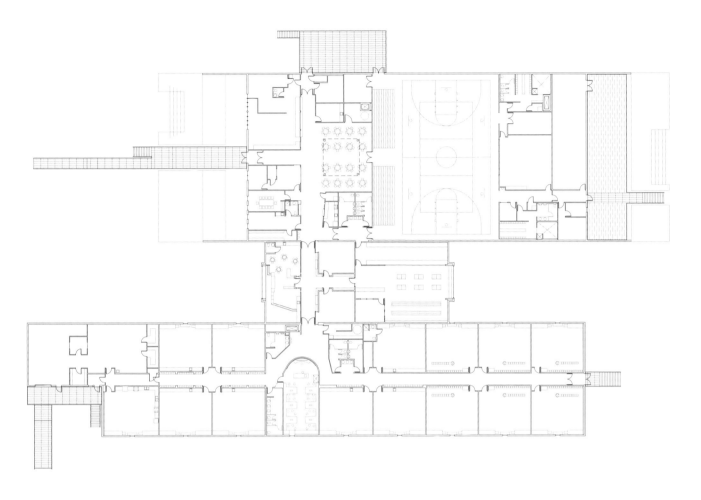

Floor plan,
Tuluksak School

project **ROVANIEMI AIRPORT**

architect **Heikkinen-Komonen Architects**
location / year Rovaniemi, Finland / 2000

Walkway leading to the airport

Through pragmatic but sweeping design elements, the architects for the Rovaniemi airport accomplished the facility's functional mission of providing gateways and ramps for air travel without neglecting its connection to the landscape. Located on the Arctic Circle, the airport takes the form of a container, or box, with a 500-foot-long external, steel-framed, curved canopy. The roads, parking lots, and terraced landscaping follow the geometry of both the building and the landscape beyond.

The fourth biggest airport in Finland—based on the number of annual passengers—the terminal sits about six miles from the city of Rovaniemi in the province of Lapland. Santa Claus Village and Santapark are located within a few miles of the terminal in Rovaniemi. Because of its unspoiled nature and numerous recreational opportunities, tourism is an important industry in Rovaniemi. Many tourists also come for the aurora borealis, or northern lights. In Finnish Lapland the number of auroral displays can be as high as two hundred per year, whereas in southern Finland the number is typically fewer than twenty.

When designing the 32,300-square-foot building, Heikkinen-Komonen Architects noted that the position of the Arctic Circle shifts depending on the Earth's axial tilt, which itself depends on tidal forces driven by the moon's orbit. North of the circle, the sun does not rise during winter solstice, nor set during summer solstice. The architects addressed this celestial phenomena with a 130-foot-long sliver of skylight parallel to the meridian of the Arctic Circle. The oblique skylight marks the circle's location during the airport's construction. The circle will reach that point again in the year 47954. In another gesture to cosmic time and movement, artist Lauri Anttila created an art installation called *Orbit of the Earth* to represent and reflect on the planet's elliptical orbit. Light coming through the ceiling at noon hits the floor in a different position every day. Over the course of a year, the pattern left by these spots of light makes a conceptual, elongated figure eight, the analemma of the sun. *Orbit of the Earth*, along with the skylight and the modern building material, counter the town's popular image as home base for Santa Claus.

Saapuvat lennot   Arrivals

The main terminal is
a box form displaying
the city's name.

Transit-matkustajat
Transitpassagerare
Transit passengers

Rovaniemi Airport

Heikkinen-Komonen Architects

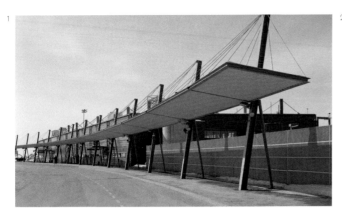

Rovaniemi Airport

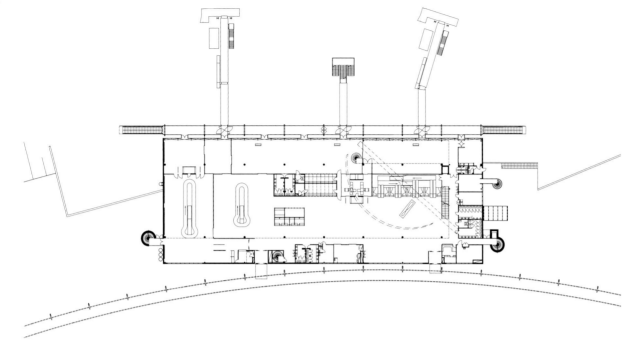

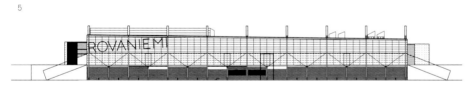

1 A 500-foot-long curved canopy defines the building's exterior.

2 Jet parked at the Rovaniemi terminal

3 An oblique skylight is a prominent element inside the terminal.

4 Floor plan

5 North elevation

latitude **78°N**
JAN. 10°F
mean
temperatures **JULY 41°F**

LONGYEARBYEN RESEARCH CENTRE, SVALBARD UNIVERSITY

project

architect **Jarmund/Vigsnæs**
location / year Svalbard, Spitzbergen, Norway / 2007

Building-concept model

Svalbard's remote location—a cluster of barren islands in the Arctic Ocean at 78°N—and its extreme climate presented a challenge to the Oslo-based architects Jarmund/Vigsnæs in designing the Longyearbyen Research Centre, a research facility located on the shores of the Advent fjord. The 91,500-square-foot polygonal complex creates an indoor campus that accommodates a rapidly growing international faculty, staff, and student body.

Svalbard University is located on the western coast of Spitzbergen, the largest island of the Svalbard archipelago. The islands support fishing and tourism as their major economic engines, among other industries. The university is the northernmost institution of higher education in the world. The city itself is one of the most northern in the world and the northernmost city with a population greater than one thousand people. In Old Norse, the name Svalbard means "the land of the cold coasts."

The Research Centre extends the existing university structure by 400 percent. Spruce-clad corridors radiate out from the atrium and adjacent public auditorium, providing access to the faculty offices,

laboratories, and classrooms for three hundred students and fifty staff in four departments of arctic study: biology, geology, geophysics, and technology. Also included in the indoor campus is the Svalbard Museum. Each corridor terminates in a gathering space with shared resources: a research library, a dining facility, large machine shops and storage areas, and the publicly accessible Svalbard History Museum exhibition hall. Like all Svalbardian buildings, the volume exists above the ground on pillars so as not to disturb the permafrost-sealed soil on which its foundations rest.

The expansive glazed aperture of the building's spruce-paneled central atrium expresses the center's mission to observe and explore the arctic environment. There is an absolute premium placed on light, thermal control, and durability in architecture built in cold climates. The insulated copper-clad skin creates an outer shell that is adjusted to the flows of wind and snow passing through the site. Climatic 3-D simulations were conducted during the design phase to ensure that the accumulation of snow would not create undesirable conditions in front of doors and windows. The main structure was

114

constructed of timbers to facilitate on-site adjustments and to avoid cold bridges. The outer copper cladding retains its workability even at low temperatures, and thereby extended the construction period further into the cold season. The separation of spaces into limbs provides the combined benefits of clear circulation and optimal natural light.

An important consideration was to create vital public spaces and passages in the building, an "interior campus" area that provides warm and lighted meeting places during the dark, cold winter. The pine-clad spaces have a complex geometry relating to the outer skin of the building. The effectiveness of circulation is maximized, but at the same time it offers varied vistas and experiences. The technical infrastructure is hidden in the tilted walls of the interior. The use of color was considered a necessity in a natural environment where colors are scarce.

The research center sits on the shores of the Advent fjord.

Longyearbyen Research Centre, Svalbard University

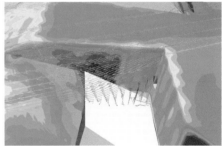

1 Skylights of the
central atrium

2 Spruce-clad stairway
leading up from the
atrium

3 The center in its
summer landscape

4 Snow study, looking
at seasonal snowfall and
drifting

5

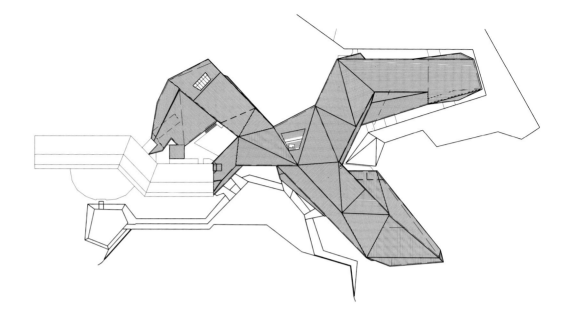

6

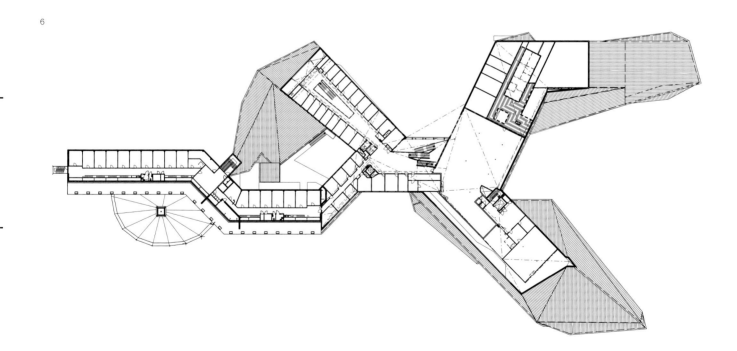

Longyearbyen Research Centre, Svalbard University

7

8

JAN. 22°F
JULY 65°F

BP
ENERGY
CENTER

project

---

architect **Koonce Pfeffer Bettis**
location / year Anchorage, Alaska / 1998

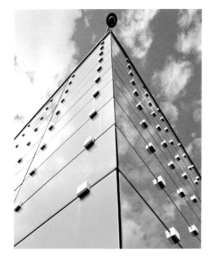

Glass facade with
construction
clamps, detail

Tucked in a small wooded area in the shadow of BP Exploration's Alaska headquarters in Anchorage, the BP Energy Center offers a secluded, cozy space for conferences, meetings, and events. Before construction the site was a swampy area populated by birch trees next to one of the city's two main highways, and was in sharp contrast to the tidy look of the huge, manicured lawns of the nearby high-rise.

While sketching and painting the setting on site, the lead designer of the project, Bruce Williams of Koonce Pfeffer-Bettis, discovered a drainage ditch covered in an area of new grass and bushes that was once Blueberry Lake. The idea of nature reclaiming itself from humankind's industrial footprint inspired him and led him to the decision to place the building at the edge of the forest away from the highway—the visitors would walk east from the parking lot, away from the parking lot, through birch trees, to arrive at the center. The noise level diminishes with each step through the woodland; as a result, the center has a retreatlike quality enhanced by the building itself.

The foliage of birch trees obscures the view of the building from the main

parking area and street during the summer. But in the winter the view through the leafless trees reveals a modern building clad in metal, with a two-story southern wing in a box form clad in panels of opaque green spandrel glass that echo the color of the birch leaves that sprout during the first two weeks of spring. The color of the building and the color of the leaves synchronize for a moment in time every year.

A form cantilevers out into the forest canopy, and windows punched through the facade provide a framed view of the birch forest—a perspective meant to stimulate contemplation rather than to distract. The patterns of Alaskan birch bark inspired the long, thin horizontal windows.

The 13,500-square-foot center offers opportunities to learn more about the energy industry through interpretive displays integrated into the facility's design. The two-story complex includes three pods, one large meeting space to the south, an exhibit space to the north, and a second floor with several smaller meeting spaces. The ground-floor pods are connected by glass corridors that also serve as exhibit spaces. The center's six meeting/conference spaces can hold anywhere from twenty to one hundred people each. One room provides a nonconventional, living-room-style space designed for informal strategic planning. Other small spaces for minimeetings are located throughout the building. An internal "pathway" ties the facility together, with small interpretive exhibits that highlight the role of energy in the Alaskan economy and culture.

The primary art installation involves a "story pipeline" in which a cross section of Alaskans tell their stories about living in the state through videotaped interviews. A screen sends the words from the interviews along an LCD ribbon that moves down the exhibit hall, through the glass out to the exterior site, and into the woods like a stream of words and red light winding through the forest.

Southeast view of spandrel-glass-clad building form

1

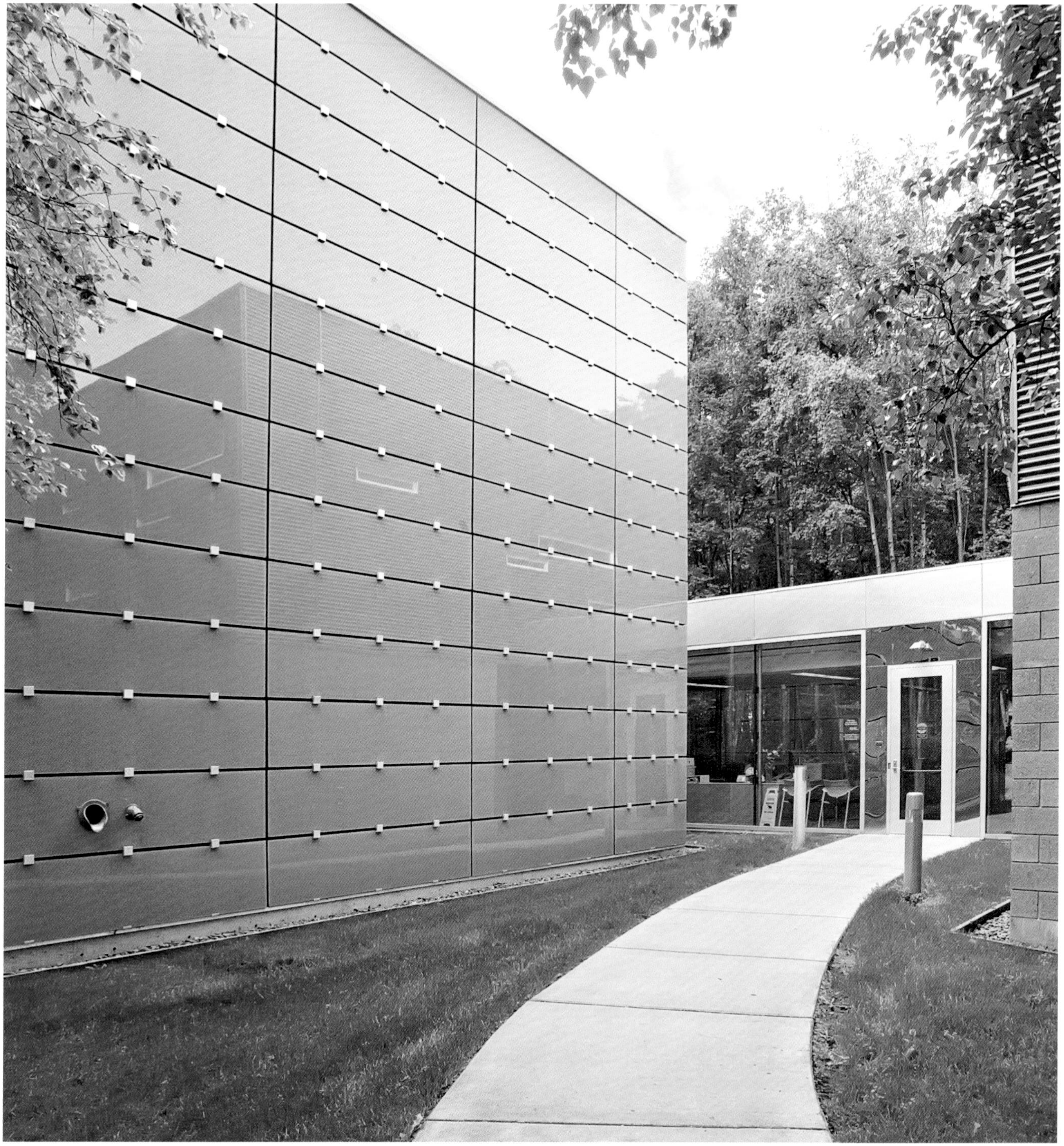

1 Approach to east entrance

2 Approach to building from the west (main parking lot) through the birch forest.

3 *Story Pipeline* runs along the north side of the building.

4 Birch trees against the northwest corner of the building facade, which is punctuated by slender horizontal windows

Koonce Pfeffer Bettis

5

FIRST SKETCH
- MANICURED LANDSCAPE FOLLOWED BY DARK FOREST
"WHAT IS INSIDE"?

6

"THIRD SKETCH
SOLUTION ARRIVED — BUILD FROM EDGE — DON'T ARRIVE + "LOOK BACK ON ARRIVAL"
—SLOW PEOPLE DOWN ! — TAKE THE JOURNEY

7

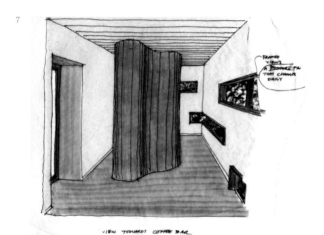

FRAMED VIEWS
A DIORAMA IN
THAT CHANGE
DAILY

VIEW TOWARDS COFFEE BAR

8

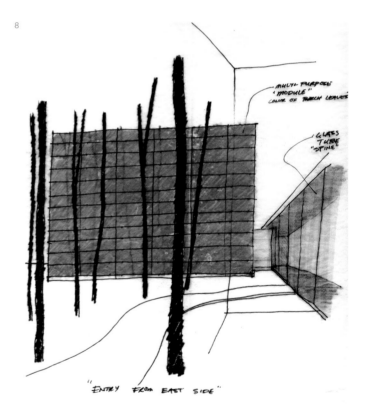

MULTI-PURPOSE "MODULE"
COLOUR OF BIRCH LEAVES

GLASS TUBE "SPINE"

"ENTRY FROM EAST SIDE"

5 Bruce Williams, watercolor sketch of surrounding birch forest

6 Bruce Williams, watercolor sketch showing approach to the site

7 Bruce Williams, watercolor showing interior building concept

8 Bruce Williams, watercolor sketch of glass-clad box and approach to building from the east

9 Second-floor plan

10 top and bottom
East elevation
West elevation

9

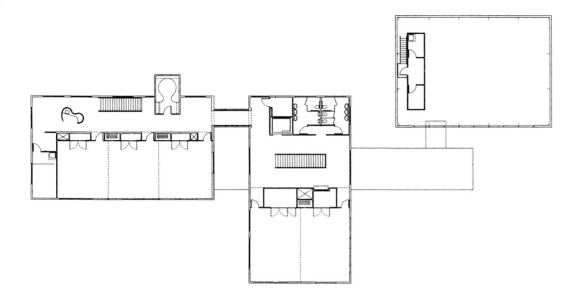

10

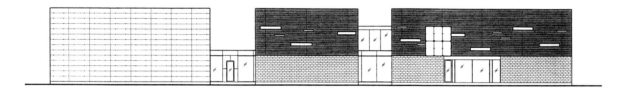

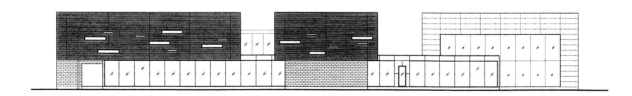

Koonce Pfeffer Bettis

latitude **64°N**
mean temperatures **JAN. -16°F**
JULY 65°F

DÄNOJÀ ZHO CULTURAL CENTRE

project

architect **Kobayashi + Zedda Architects**
location / year Dawson City, Yukon, Canada / 1998

Wood structures and slats suggest indigenous structures, the surrounding forests, fish baskets and drying racks, and other traditional references.

Designed by Kobayashi + Zedda Architects of Whitehorse, Yukon, in Canada, the Dänojà Zho Cultural Centre reaffirms and celebrates the traditional home of the Tr'ondëk Hwëch'in along the Yukon River, the great traveling route and source of salmon.

Perched upon a dyke, the center links the river with historic Dawson City. In a symbolic gesture of conciliation between the first inhabitants and those who arrived over a century ago, the building highlights the presence of the great river and provides a place of gathering, a place of dance, storytelling, and the collecting and showing of artifacts. Its exhibits are a guide through the story of life at the traditional fish camp of Tr'ondëk, the gold rush, and the steps the Tr'ondëk Hwëch'in took to become a self-governing nation.

The structure of the building recognizes both the traditional and contemporary living culture of the Tr'ondëk Hwëch'in with references to traditional natural wood-built structures, such as the traditional winter shelters built of timber (referenced through angled wood slats that dominate the building's exterior) and salmon-drying racks, alongside steel and glass. The building is also oriented to the river, the lifeline of the indigenous culture—as it would be in traditional Tr'ondëk Hwëch'in positioning of structures.

1 Building entrance
with Yukon River in
background

2 A walkway runs
between the building and
the Yukon River.

127

3

4

5

Dänojà Zho Cultural Centre

6

3 View of the center from across the Yukon River

4 Building entrance

5 Wood is layered on both the interior and exterior of the building.

6 Interior lobby

7 Front desk near entrance, with windows allowing views out to the Yukon River

7

EXIT

EXIT

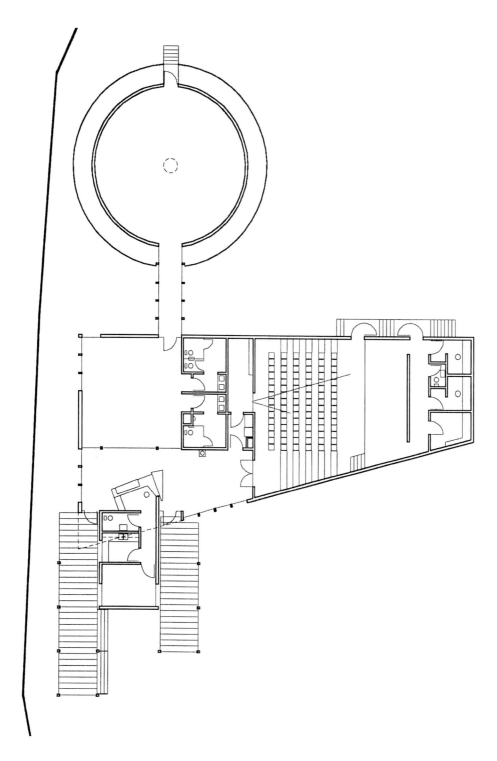

Dänojà Zho Cultural Centre

9

8 Floor plan

9 West elevation

10 Section

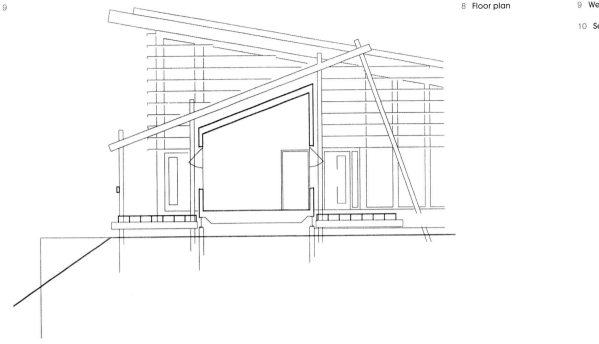

10

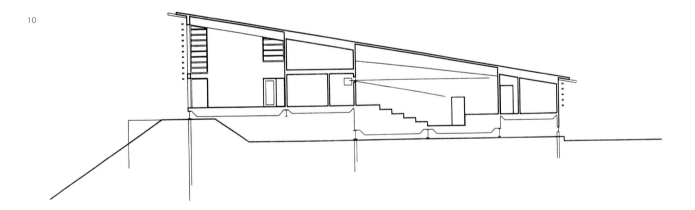

Kobayashi + Zedda Architects

131

latitude **61°N**
JAN. 22°F
mean
temperatures **JULY 65°F**

project
NEARPOINT HOUSE

architect **Workshop for Architecture and Design**
location / year Anchorage, Alaska / 2009

Exterior decking provides additional access to views on the west (Cook Inlet) and north (Alaska Range) sides of the home.

Situated on a short ridge at the base of the Chugach Mountains, the Nearpoint house offers expansive views of the Alaska Range to the north, and downtown Anchorage and the Cook Inlet to the west. A clearing made for an unrealized house that had been previously planned for the property provided a natural location for this private home in a birch grove.

Workshop for Architecture and Design focused on four primary design concerns: creating specific landscape and social relationships that would be transformed as the occupants inhabited different areas of the home and site; direct access to landscape and exterior spaces; exploration of the differing relationship between use and thermal performance; and environmental responsibility.

At the beginning of the design phase, the client sent a postcard to design architect Steve Bull with a short list of values to be embodied in the house, which included energy and environmental responsibility, timeless and durable construction, ability to house an eclectic mix of art and collections, respect for nature, sense of community, simplicity, and a creative use of space. The

architects responded by creating a clean interior volume with open living spaces that share in all communal activity. Private spaces within the home are modest, bringing the emphasis back to the shared spaces and family life.

Disturbance of the exterior site was minimal, and the landscape is a dominant feature of the home. By orienting the house horizontally along the site's ridge, the architects ensured that the structure relates to the forest understory as well as to the broad panorama beyond. Interior elements like the use of wide, high windows coupled with low horizontal ones emphasize this scope of magnification. In this way, the house extends along the rise like a path with views and connections to both the near and distant landscapes, grounding the owners to the foliage and topography of the site as well as the vast wilderness around it.

132

West facade

Nearpoint House

North facade with
Chugach Mountains in
the distance

Workshop for Architecture and Design

Nearpoint House

1 A corridor separates main living areas from private spaces.

2 Kitchen. Clerestory windows allow for exposure to the precious natural light coming from the south.

3 Main living area

4 A loft space offers additional square footage.

5 Kitchen, with views to the west

6

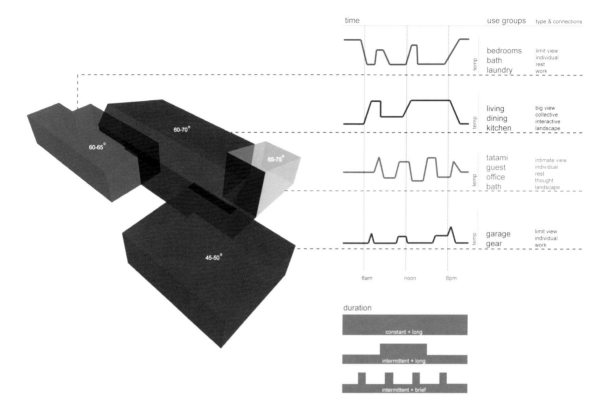

time		use groups	type & connections

60-65°
60-70°
65-75°

45-50°

temp | bedrooms bath laundry | limit view individual rest work

temp | living dining kitchen | big view collective interactive landscape

temp | tatami guest office bath | intimate view individual rest thought landscape

temp | garage gear | limit view individual work

6am   noon   6pm

duration

constant + long

intermittent + long

intermittent + brief

7

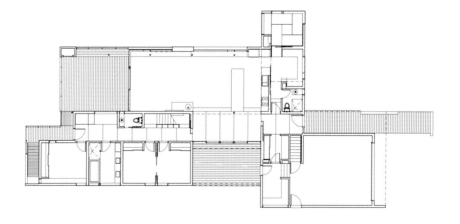

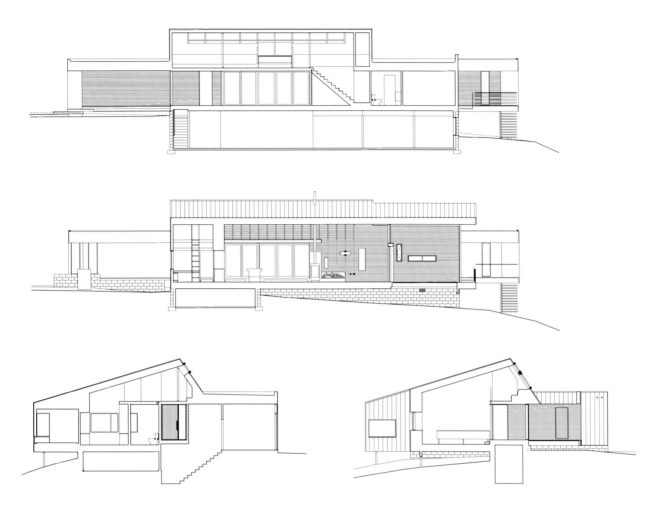

6 Thermal zoning plan, an energy-conservation study. Thermal zoning is the subdivision of spaces inside the building that have varying thermal temperatures.

7 Floor plan

8 clockwise from top
North section
South section
East section
West section

project **HOF RESIDENCE**

architect **Studio Granda**
location / year Skagafjörður fjord, Iceland / 2007

Arial view. The displaced grass of the field reappears on the roof, and removed meadowland shows up in cut and folded earthworks of turf and stone that open ways to the entrance and terraces.

The new Hof residence joins an existing assemblage of structures consisting of a house, church, barn, and cowshed on a riverbank in the Skagafjörður fjord in Iceland, less than sixty miles from the Arctic Circle. The wide fjord, with a mountainous rim, embraces the cliff islands of Drangey and Málmey, along with the foreland, Thordahofdi (Þórðarhöfði).

The 3,170-square-foot house sits on higher ground, slightly removed from the older cluster of buildings. The design by Studio Granda honors the integrity of the landscape through the use of materials. Hexagonal basalt pillars excavated from the site during preparation of the foundation were used to pave the external walkways; the application of this same stone in the living and circulation areas created textural continuity. Telegraph poles salvaged from the site were remade into a sun/privacy screen on the south-facing windows, and the field grass removed during site preparation was reused on the roof. Even meadowland pulled out during site work was repurposed in entrance areas and terraces.

The house rises from the grassy site with a sheer cedar and concrete facade that will weather over time. The vertical cedar boards seem to mimic the earthen hue of the mountains. Smooth interior walls of raw or painted concrete offset the rustic palette created by oiled oak ceilings, doors, and other carpentry. Marble surfaces take on a refined look in the bathroom and kitchen, but a larder glazed with white tiles and equipped with basalt shelves serves as a reminder of the need to stash food for harsh winters.

The house is highly insulated and thermally stable due to the massive concrete walls, stone floors, and balanced fenestration. Geothermal water is used for the floor heating and radiators as well as for all domestic use. What little electricity is required to run the home comes from hydroelectric and geothermal sources.

The house offers dramatic views while welcoming natural light from a secondary system of clerestory lights and other penetrations in the ceiling. Only the route between the living area and bedrooms gets reduced to just a few pinpricks of light.

1 View from the west

2 Natural stones from the
site create a courtyard
between the wings
of the structure.

Hof Residence

6

3 The exterior of sheer cedar and concrete walls will slowly weather based on the vagaries of climate.

4 The vertical cedar boards define the exterior.

5 View out from corridor leading to main living area

6 Wood, stone, and concrete are the materials used in the main living area.

7 Main living area

7

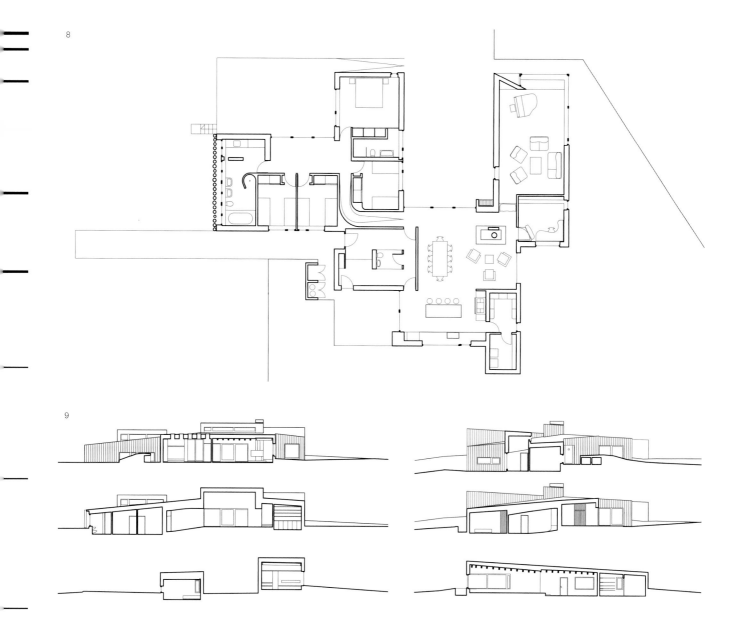

8

9

Hof Residence

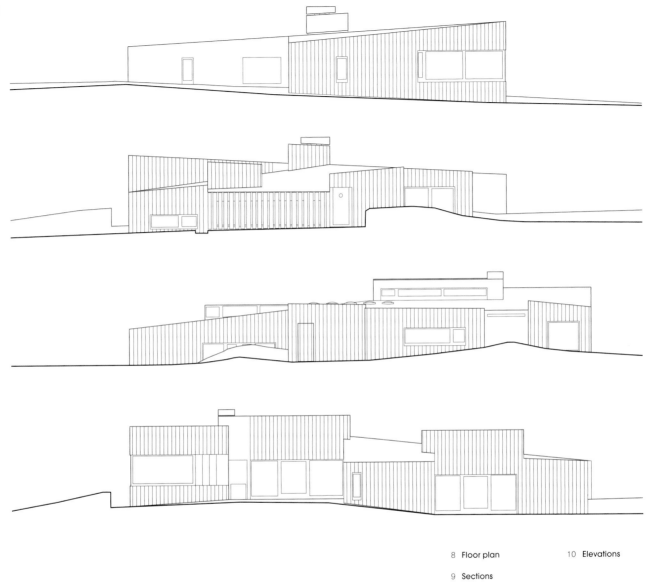

10

8 Floor plan   10 Elevations

9 Sections

Studio Granda

latitude **67°N**
JAN.-30°F
mean
temperatures **JULY 65°F**

project
OLD CROW VISITOR'S CENTER

architect **Kobayashi + Zedda Architects**
location / year Old Crow, Yukon Territory, Canada / 2008

Some visitors arrive
to the visitor's center
by small plane.

Old Crow is a small town of about three hundred aboriginal people known as the Vuntut Gwitchin, and is located at the confluence of the Crow and Porcupine rivers at 67° latitude. The visitor's center designed by Kobayashi + Zedda Architects sits along the Porcupine River and near the Old Crow town site, and is oriented toward the culturally important Porcupine River and in a southern direction for maximum solar exposure.

The center—the building concept of which evolved from a simple sketch of an outline of a caribou antler—is an identifiable icon. A sloping building section both shields the building from northeasterly winds and visually connects the building occupants to the river and the south exposure. A long linear outdoor deck overlooks the river, extends the interior interpretive/reception areas to the outside, and will accommodate a future connection to both outdoor exhibit components and the river. A 4.3 kW grid-tied photovoltaic array, an application of solar cells for energy use, is paired with translucent panels to provide both shading and up to 7 percent of the building's annual electrical needs. As Old Crow's electricity is supplied by diesel generators,

the photovoltaic array helps offset the transportation and fuel cost to run the generators. Additionally, costs associated with building construction and material transportation also impacted the building concept. The simple and elegant design solution minimized material usage and maximized the greatest opportunity for construction by local labor. The open design also allows for a mezzanine area to be used for general storage and mechanical systems. This helps reduce the building footprint and construction costs, and consolidating and centralizing mechanical systems allows for double-height spaces in key building component areas (exhibit area, theater, reception, and gift shop).

The building is made of structural insulated-panels (SIPs) in which the insulation material is packaged between boards that allow the whole unit to serve as a structural building material. SIPs allow for quick erection on-site and minimize material transportation costs and material wastage on site. A system of segmented truss ribs forms the main structural skeleton. This allows sufficient cavity size for high levels of insulation (R-60, or a three-star energy efficiency rating), typical for roof, wall, and floor assemblies. The structural system of rib trusses is clad with the SIP panels to provide necessary thermal protection and to reduce shearing. The structural system is clad with one-by-four pine slats on the interior surface to limit the requirement for gypsum wall-board. The exterior skin is clad with horizontal cement board/corrugated steel siding, which is low in maintenance and high in durability. Extensive canopies constructed of turned-logs (logs with the bark and branches removed) occur at the building deck and at entry areas. Ample windows dominate the south elevation. In addition to providing important natural light, the windows provide a good view of the Porcupine River and beyond. Natural lighting in the exhibit areas includes indirect clerestory-level glazing, making the building open, transparent, and well connected to its natural site.

The center expresses the culture of the Vuntut Gwitchin First Nation and the majestic quality of the land in Vuntut National Park.

South facade with building entrance

148   Old Crow Visitor's Center

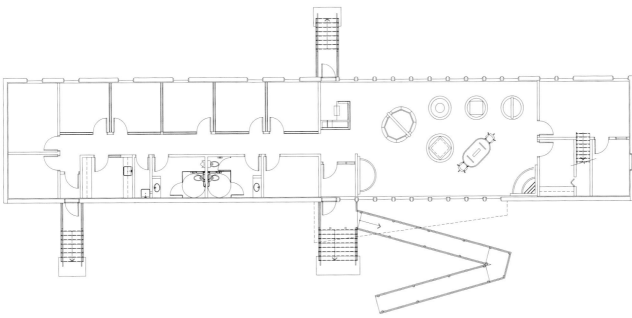

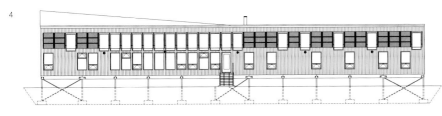

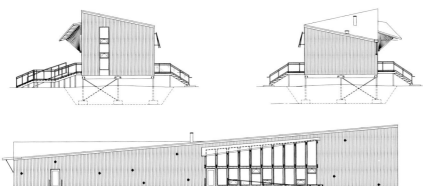

1 Interior housing permanent and temporary exhibitions, with windows that allow in light from the south

2 Exhibition space

3 Floor plan

4 Elevations

Kobayashi + Zedda Architects

project **PHELPS/ BURKE RESIDENCE**

architect **mayer sattler-smith**
location / year Anchorage, Alaska / 2004

West facade

Phelps/Burke Residence in south Anchorage is designed to maximize the view of Fire Island to the west and the mudflats and the volcanic range to the south. The house's vantage point provides an ideal place to watch a dynamic landscape endlessly altered by the extreme tides and climate of Cook Inlet. Ten-foot ceiling heights and floor-to-ceiling windows emphasize these perspectives while enhancing light and transparency.

The house sits on a pie-shaped lot—less than ideal for a traditional house—with a narrow footprint influenced by the clients' and architects' desire to spare two mature trees during construction. Though limited by these site constraints, the house's east-west orientation takes advantage of the southern exposure. Because the occupants spend a lot of time out of state, they also wanted to be able to easily close up the house for long periods of time. They suggested a design based on shipping containers. With that in mind, the design embraces box forms and makes use of composite-material siding traditionally used for decking, largely in response to the clients' desire for a no-maintenance solution.

Concrete floors offer a contemporary feel and continue the low- to no-maintenance approach. The public living space occupies the second floor of the house with a structural fireplace and eating nook off the kitchen. Wall-sized windows bring the outdoors in through light and a sense of open space. Windows on the east side of the top floor can roll back like barn doors, allowing greater integration of the outdoors.

The lower floor combines work space, bedrooms, and a guest room with movable partitions that allow one room to flow into the next or be closed off for privacy. These lower-floor bedrooms also offer seclusion from noise caused by high winds common to the region.

Outside spaces include a covered deck on the south and west sides of the upper level, as well as a north deck that offers a wind-sheltered space with a fireplace and barbeque. An elevated fifteen-foot-by-fifteen-foot studio, separate from the house, has twelve-foot ceilings and provides a quiet space for creating artwork or listening to music.

South facade

1

1 West facade with
Cook Inlet to the south

2 South facade

3 Kitchen with
living area beyond

4 View from main living
area out to Cook Inlet

5 Main living area

2

Phelps/Burke Residence

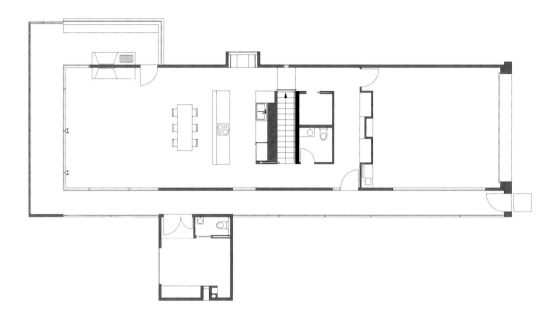

Upper-floor plan

Lower-floor plan

MAASSEN/ GOUWENS RESIDENCE

project

architect **Black + White Studio Architects**
location / year Anchorage, Alaska / 2009

Freestanding building with separate garage and recreation room

The Maassen/Gouwens Residence, designed by Anchorage-based Black + White Studio Architects, puts its occupants into a visceral relationship with the Chugach Mountains and an outdoor lifestyle. The building sits on a four-acre plot of land in between a mountain range and a valley—what the architects saw as a place of transition—with a creek running through the back side of the property. In this way, the house exists in transition as well—both in and out of the hill at the same time.

A detached garage—which many consider unusual or undesirable in the subarctic climate—serves as the entrance to the property. Though Anchorage residents depend on the automobile because of the vastness of the city limits and a lack of public transportation, the architects wanted to demonstrate that once you separate the automobile from the place you live, it opens up the possibilities for architecture. A pathway leads away from the garage and past a small office, a guest room, and then the main house, creating a mix of structures with outdoor transition areas. Underneath the garage a recreation room provides a separate but connected space for teenagers.

Lights lead from this garage/recreation area to the courtyard of the main house along a path that descends along the natural fall line of the hill.

Expansive views dominate the 3,300-square-foot home, and exposed timbers and ash wood floors in the living areas give it a spacious, woodsy look. Overall, the house is bright and light, particularly the kitchen, where natural light comes in from all directions. Horses are kept on the property and can be seen from the bedrooms, while two decks offer different experiences—one exposed to the elements for brilliant nights and warm summer days and the other as a covered shelter from the rain and snow. A rooftop garden offers a lookout from which to view an expanse of alders, the city of Anchorage in the distance, and Cook Inlet beyond. Moose, bears, and small animals wander along the creek line as well.

1 Freestanding garage on right and entry building to main living area on left

2 West facade on a winter night

Maassen/Gouwens Residence

Black + White Studio Architects

Maassen/Gouwens Residence

1 Entry to main living area

2 View from north into main living area

3 Second-floor master bedroom with translucent glass framing the stair

4 left and right
Second-floor plan
First-floor plan

4

BIRCH HILL SKI BUILDING

project

architect **Bettisworth North**
location / year Fairbanks, Alaska / 2003

Roof canopy, detail

Nordic ski teams from the United States and other countries compete and train in the world-class Birch Hill recreation area a few miles northeast of Fairbanks. The downhill area is surrounded by miles of cross-country trails, including six miles of lighted trails for night skiing in "the land of the midnight sun." Diehard skiers still love to hit the trails on the slopes, even in Fairbanks, where temperatures dip to -65°F or colder. Competitive cross-country skiers believe the area has the best early-season snow in the United States.

The 11,175-square-foot ski building fulfills the Birch Hill mission through a service pod clad in galvanized metal, consisting of an entryway, an elevator, a stairway, waxing areas, changing rooms, and bathrooms. The second pod, which serves as a warming shelter and public gathering area, looks warmer and less industrial because of its cedar wood siding. These pods are connected to each other with a viewing bridge, which spans the incoming ski trail. (The trail is used recreationally and also serves as a trail for local, state, and international ski competitions.)

The wood structure is revealed, rather than covered with siding or drywall, both outside at the bridge and inside in the assembly pod, creating a rustic character commonly associated with ski venues. The material and color selections provide a bright and colorful backdrop to stadium activities and the white of winter. From the interior, there are views out to the slopes; seen from outside on the trails, the interior provides a beacon for skiers in the darkness.

Painted cedar siding
serves as cladding on
the warming shelter and
public gathering area of
the ski building.

1 Main entrance

2 Viewing bridge span-
ning the ski trail and connecting the two building
pods

3 View of facade from
downhill side

4 View of ski complex
from the west

Birch Hill Ski Building

Bettisworth North

Birch Hill Ski Building

5 Interior of main entrance

6 Corridor

7 Interior of
viewing bridge

8 clockwise from top left
West elevation
East elevation
South elevation
North elevation

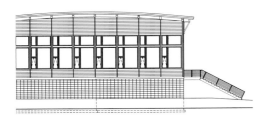

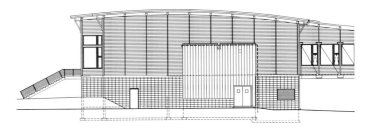

LAUGALÆKJARSKÓL SECONDARY SCHOOL ADDITION

project

architect **Studio Granda**
location / year Reykjavik, Iceland / 2004

The Laugalækjarskóli Secondary School Addition connects two identical three-story school buildings built in the 1960s: one perpendicular to the addition and the other parallel to it. The new structure connects the two buildings in the middle to form an L-shaped complex. Studio Granda designed the addition to connect at the ground floor in order to reduce the visual impact of the new structure. The firm also designed an expanded rooftop with several levels and environments. Rooftop walkways link the addition to the school's original entrances, for example, and the use of grass on the upper roof areas reinforces the idea of the roof as landscaping. The design also minimizes the apparent mass of the new 10,500-square-foot extension by giving it a relatively low profile and using the roof for walkways and landscaping. These choices keep the addition from gaining visual domi-nance over the existing buildings.

The exterior walls of the addition replicate the facades of neighborhood build-ings. At the same time, the subtle twist of the grass roof hints at the geometry of the period. Internally, the twist mediates between the different functions of the addition. From the lofty hall, the ceiling slopes down via a voluminous entrance to a horizontally accented library.

The central connecting corridor rises to double height and has a series of generous skylights that reveal glimpses of natural light, the weather, and activity taking place on the upper walkway. Internal surfaces continue the original material palette of linoleum, oak, and glossy paint.

Approach toward main
entrance

Laugalækjarskóli Secondary School Addition

1 The roof features walkways.

2 Rooftop walkways link the various spaces of the complex.

3 The skylights of the double-height central connecting corridor offer glimpses toward the sky and of activity on the upper walkway.

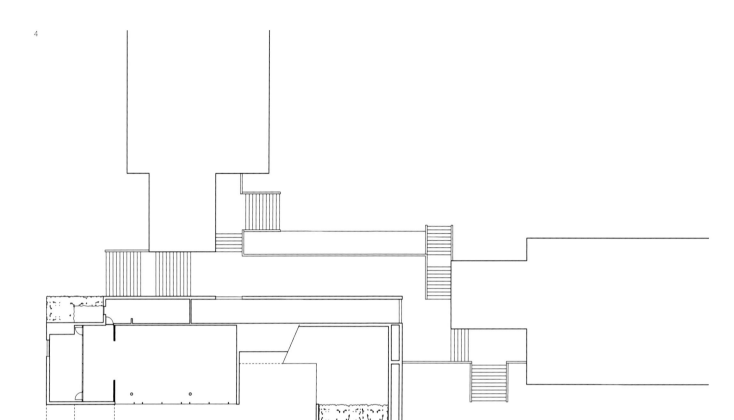

4

5

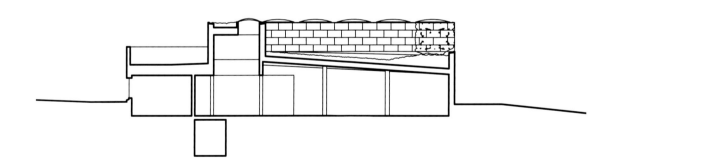

Laugalækjarskóli Secondary School Addition

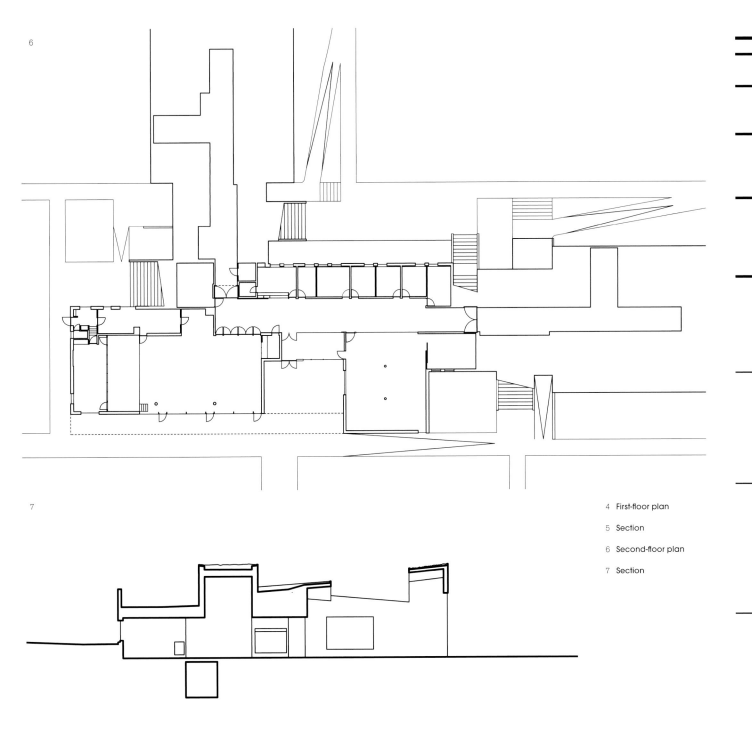

6

7

4 First-floor plan

5 Section

6 Second-floor plan

7 Section

project

TANTALUS SCHOOL

architect **Kobayashi + Zedda Architects**
location / year Carmacks, Yukon, Canada / 2007

Carmacks is a picturesque community located at the confluence of the Nordenskiold and Yukon rivers in northern Canada, about two hours north of Whitehorse. Called Tantalus in the 1800s, it is now known as the Hub of the Yukon, because almost any destination in the Yukon can be accessed easily by road from the small city. The population of Carmacks is approximately 520 people.

The new Tantalus School, designed by Kobayashi + Zedda Architects, accommodates about one hundred elementary and secondary students, almost 85 percent with First Nations ancestry. The first school building, the Roadhouse, was built in 1903 and had three large rooms and a dining room that seated about forty people. The new school, adjacent to the Klondike Highway, is equipped with a full shop and a state-of-the-art computer room, which complements its unique technology education program. There is a dedicated native language room for use with the K-12 Native Language Program.

The published *Architectural Request For Proposal* mandated a First Nations cultural response to the architectural program. Overwhelmingly, First Nations members felt that a circular scheme would be an appropriate symbolic gesture to their cultural

traditions. During the development phase, the circular scheme was replaced by a segmented-arcing scheme in order to work within the available construction budget while maintaining the rounded gesture.

The energy performance of the building was an important consideration, and the school's orientation on the site was determined to maximize penetration of diffused daylight while minimizing solar gain. The east-west orientation faces the town and is perpendicular to southern daylight. Views of the surrounding mountains and the nearby Yukon River were limited because of the forest and distance to the surrounding hills, but the curve in the river provided the inspiration for the arc of the school.

The primary architectural feature of the school is the multipurpose room adjacent to the main entrance. Its circle-based form and sunscreen is loosely based on the concept of the traditional moose skin hut—stretched and tanned moose hides pulled over a wood frame. The exterior frame consists of curved cedar ribs laid out in segments to form a semicircular sunscreen around the room's main windows. Inside, bent wood trim and circular flooring patterns help enhance the circularity of the space. The upper horizontal strip windows of the multipurpose room in the gray portion of the building evoke the arc of the sun during a typical day.

An important aspect of the livable design is the maximum availability of daylight to all rooms. This was achieved through high clerestory windows. The classrooms have sloping ceilings as well, allowing all rooms to get the benefit of southern diffused light, no matter what their location. All ceilings are either white or of Galvalume to maximize light reflection. State-of-the-art glazing material selectively admits only light in the visible range of the spectrum, thus avoiding heat loss or gain through infrared transmission. Protection from the direct summer sun and diffusion of southern daylight is achieved by sunshades or light shelves designed for the particular sun angles in Carmacks.

The choice of methods and materials throughout the design and construction of the school was determined by function, soundness, economy, aesthetics, and the benefit to Yukon businesses and workers.

View toward main entrance

Tantalus School

West facade

Kobayashi + Zedda Architects

1 Exterior of multipur-
pose room

2 Windows open to let
fresh air into classrooms.

3 Windows continue
the circular theme of the
building.

4 View from interior
corridor

1

Tantalus School

Kobayashi + Zedda Architects

5

Tantalus School

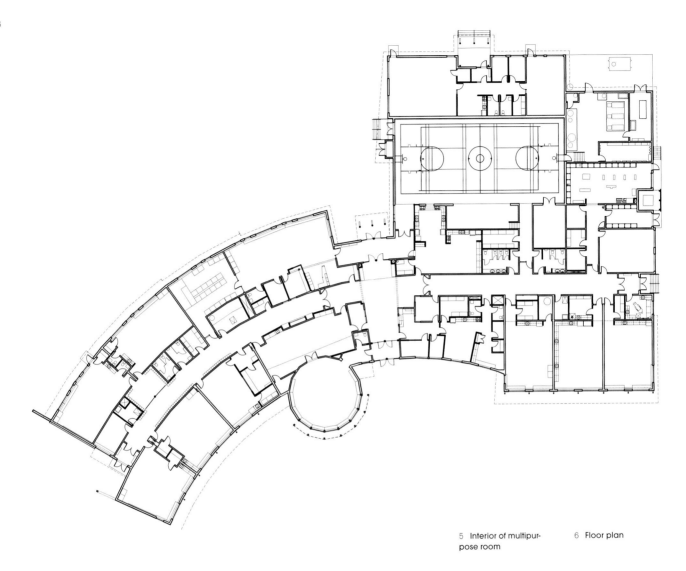

5 Interior of multipur-
pose room

6 Floor plan

project

MOUNTAIN CABIN

architect **div.A Architects**
location / year Hemsedal, Norway / 2007

Main entrance

The approximately 5,000-square-foot lodge designed by div.A Architects is close to the Hemsedal ski resort, making it easy for visitors to ski to and from the lodge and the slopes. The layout of the chalet reflects the desire to maximize the number of beds while establishing a single common area with a kitchen and dining and living rooms. All bedrooms have dramatic views of the mountain, and a large concrete fireplace serves as the main attraction in the interior. The concrete fireplace and built-in wood stove are modern interpretations of the traditional Norwegian fireplace and act as the main heat source. The large, solid oak dining table with solid oak benches makes a clear reference to traditional Norwegian farm-kitchen furniture.

The building has a very simple footprint and uses a simple palette of materials. The chalet is built with a combination of timber and concrete and uses the contrast of materials—the wooden box inside the concrete frame—as architectural elements. All horizontal timber surfaces are in oak, and all vertical wooden surfaces are in black-stained spruce or black medium-density fiberboard.

Approach to main
entrance

Mountain Cabin

5

1 Site plan

2 Exterior walkway. Canopy prevents snow buildup along building.

3 Front facade with horizontal oak timbers and vertical black-stained spruce

4 Kitchen

5 Main living area

div.A Architects

185

MOUNTAIN LODGE

project

architect **Helen & Hard**
location / year The Pulpit Rock, Lyse Fjord, Norway / 2009

Exterior wall and roof
construction, detail

The Pulpit Rock Mountain Lodge, the winning design-competition entry (2004) by Helen & Hard, accommodates twenty-eight guest rooms, a cafe, a restaurant, and a conference room. The lodge is situated at the trailhead leading to The Pulpit Rock, the sheer cliff cantilevering over the Lyse Fjord. The lodge's placement and mass befits the immediate environment with its undulating terrain and rock outcropping around which the lodge's volume is bent. The building is partly hidden from the parking areas to the north by the natural terrain formation.

The client is Stavanger Turistforening (Stavanger Trekking Association), an association that facilitates hiking in the mountains through small public cabins. It needed a new building to serve the rapidly increasing amount of tourists going to visit The Pulpit Rock (120,000 a year). Furthermore, the old cabin, which was built in 1947 with bunk beds and a shared shower in the hallway, did not meet modern standards. The new accommodation will have upgraded bathroom facilities, a restaurant with a capacity of one hundred guests, and a small conference room, yet remain modest. Stavanger Turistforening also requested that

the building be built with environmentally friendly materials.

The construction system consists of thirty-two wooden ribs of massive timber elements placed about nine feet apart. Every wall, the floor, and the roof were built with the same prefabricated system. The ribs are doubled up in between the guest rooms to avoid lateral sound transfer. The ribs are hollowed out to increase spaciousness in public areas. The massive timbers are made of a system called Holz100, selected because it involves completely wooden construction without glue or nails

Construction materials included only wood, stone, steel, glass, and concrete. Massive timber walls are insulated with recycled newspapers on the outside, covered with a wood-fiber plate coupled with cladding in pine-core wood.

1 View of entry from parking lot

2 Front facade

187

Mountain Lodge

Helen & Hard

7

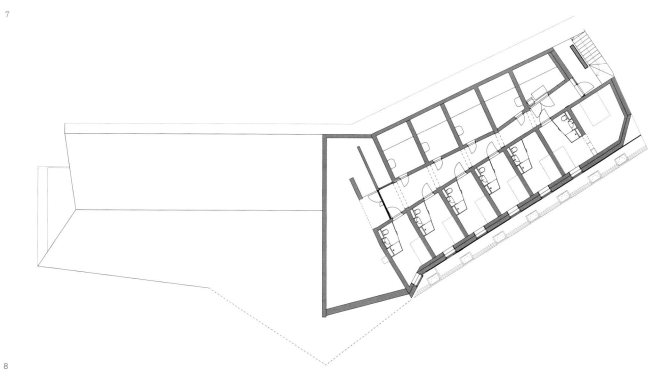

8

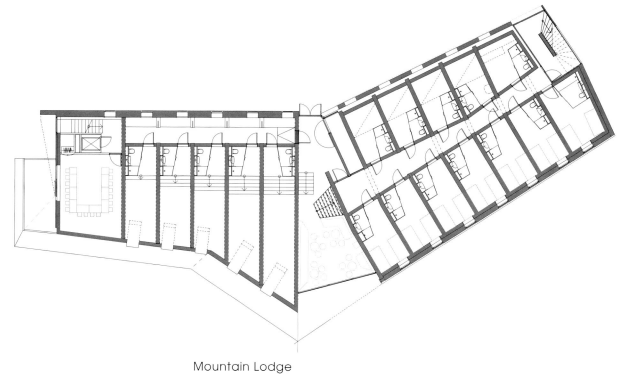

Mountain Lodge

9

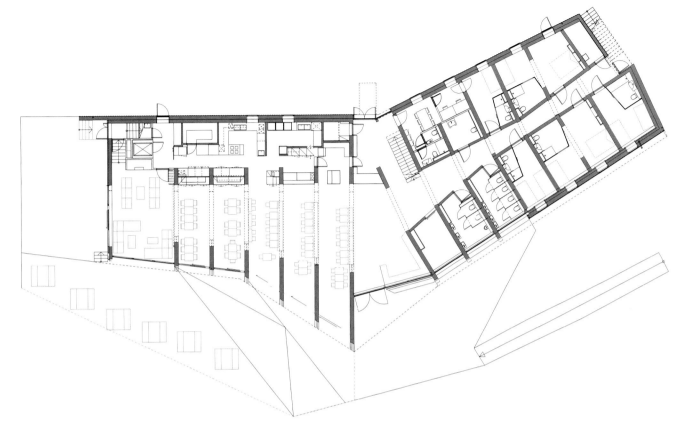

10

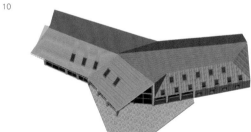

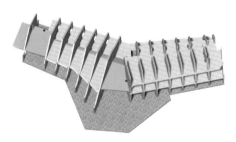

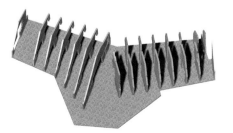

7 Third-floor plan

8 Second-floor plan

9 First-floor plan

10 clockwise from top left
3-D sections:
Aerial view
Second-floor view
Ground-floor view
First-floor view

Helen & Hard

project **SUMMERHOUSE**

architect **Saunders and Wilhelmsen**
location / year Aaland, Finland / 2002

Front entrance

Tommie Wilhelmsen and Todd Saunders live and work in Bergen, Norway's second-largest city. Wilhelmsen is Norwegian, but Saunders emigrated from Canada. In 1998 the two paired up to teach a six-week course at the Bergen Architecture School and discovered shared ideas, working styles, and career aspirations. Their first projects centered on themselves as client, including this summerhouse on the edge of a fjord.

The summerhouse takes an ecologically ambitious approach to function and design through materials like linseed fiber insulation and a wood exterior treated with natural oils. The wood for the house came from a local sawmill, and the home was built on pillars to avoid the removal of roots or trees.

The house consists of two structures connected by an outdoor room with a long roof. This rooftop above the two buildings shelters users from the frequent rain on the west coast of Finland. The structure is disarmingly simple and restrained. It incorporates nature as a room connecting two buildings, the whole structure situated on the edge of a pristine pine forest, on top of a rocky slope.

The two structures of the home are connected by an outdoor "room."

Summerhouse

4

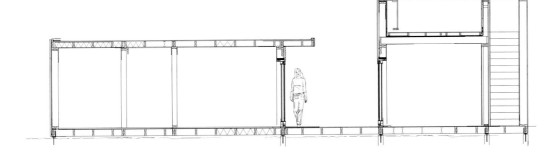

5

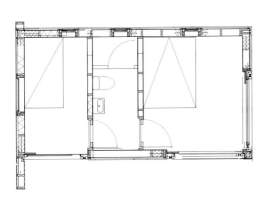
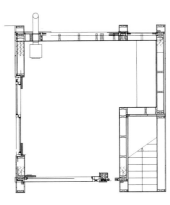

6

1 The roof offers views of
the surroundings.

2 Stairway access to roof

3 View of back of home.
The wood for the house
came from a local
sawmill.

4 South elevation

5 Floor plan

6 top and bottom
South elevation
North elevation

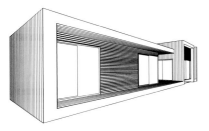

project **DAVIS RESIDENCE**

architect **Black + White Studio Architects**
location / year Anchorage, Alaska / 2009

South facade with access to backyard and view into kitchen

This addition and renovation of a private residence pays homage to the existing 1950s ranch-style home; half of the original building was kept largely intact, including its interior, with a modern expansion added to the east side on top of the original foundation. The addition emphasizes contemporary design, public spaces, and contact with nature. The site is in a neighborhood that used to be considered the edge of the city but now nestles at the edge of downtown. Most residents now live to the south of it.

Architects Bruce Williams and Michael Gerace created spaces with large northern and southern windows, with views of the street, along with a private backyard on the south side to take advantage of the southern exposure, the source of the warm sun in the subarctic climate. A large tree in the front yard increases privacy amid the urban landscape, and stadium-sized steps at the back of the house lead gently from the kitchen to outdoor places where the family can sit, eat lunch, and spend time with a surprising amount of privacy. Despite the contemporary nature of the addition, the home still respects the neighborhood vernacular. In particular, the scale of the

home is appropriate to the surrounding homes, and the chimney design reflects those of the neighboring houses.

Natural light plays an important role in the home, with large windows carefully placed for transparency and southern exposure. A skylight in the kitchen opens views to a pine tree that extends from the backyard far above the house. The uniqueness of the Alaskan latitude means that the homeowners do not need to turn on many lights between April and August, when days are long. At the same time, the quality of artificial light is very important during winter, when interior lights are essential.

Even the basement gets natural light, from exterior openings that allow occupants to see out and light to enter. During winter, these windows remove the potentially claustrophobic effect of the low seven foot, three inch basement ceilings.

Davis Residence

Black + White Studio Architects

Davis Residence

4

1 Kitchen and
main living area

2 View from kitchen
toward main living area

3 View south from
main entry

4 Kitchen

5 Original floor plan for
existing home

6 North elevation

5

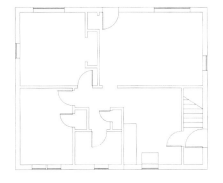

6

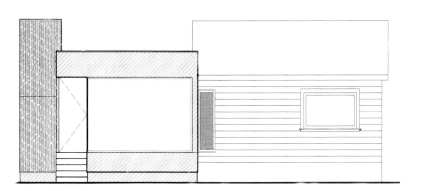

MITTON RESIDENCE

project

architect **Black + White Studio Architects**

location / year Anchorage, Alaska / 2009

Concept study

This remodeling of an existing home shows what can be done when confronted with suburbia in the North: the proliferation of contractor-spec homes in the subarctic that results from an effort to economize.

The Mitton family hired Bruce Williams and Michael Gerace of Black + White Studio Architects to add on to their Anchorage home: a split-level built in the 1970s when Anchorage was booming from oil revenues and the housing market exploded. Though not their dream home, the house did have a big yard with a garden and made it convenient to get to work and city amenities. The back of the house also had a great southern exposure.

The goal of the remodel was to allow for growing room for four children, some entering their teenage years, and to construct a space in which the kids could be creative. The addition is a rectangular cube that sits on top of the garage at the front of the house. It gives the children a place to sleep, work, and explore via a long space that can turn into two rooms with a sliding divider door. The front wall takes advantage of the mountain view by alternating vertical cabinetry with floor-to-ceiling etched glass

behind built-in shelving and desks. Windows to the north and south of the addition swing out on different pivot points to maximize the air currents.

Finish materials are simple and functional, but warm and appropriate to the North. Alaskan yellow cedar is applied on the walls, floors, and ceilings and is visible from the exterior, with spots of color to give the space life. Large windows keep the small spaces from feeling closed-in and maximize the opportunity for light.

The addition is divided and delineated from the existing house through materials. The wood floor of the addition contrasts with the carpet of the house, for example, but each relates to the other through the relationships of its occupants.

View from the street

Milton Residence

6

1 Street view, in context
with the neighborhood

2 Work/study space

3 Work space,
with view to the street

4 Work/study space with
side windows allowing for
natural light through the
length of the space.

5 Work spaces with
lighting in the floor
marking separation
between spaces

6 Bedroom with shared
work space beyond

7 Floor plan

8 South elevation

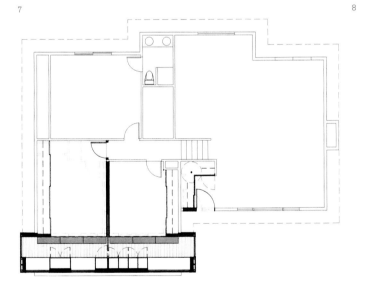

7

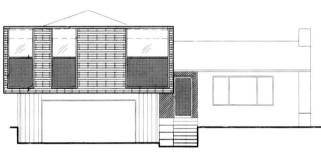

8

latitude **53°N**
JAN. 12°F
mean
temperatures **JULY 64°F**

MOORELANDS CAMP DINING HALL

project

architect **Shim-Sutcliffe Architects**
location / year Kawagama Lake, Dorset, Ontario / 2002

Corner detail

The northern Ontario landscape is filled with lakes, remote islands, and peninsulas heavily laden with pine trees and strewn with large rocks. It is on one of these peninsulas that Moorelands Camp is located, accessible only by crossing Kawagama Lake by boat. The nonprofit camp is an annual summer destination for economically disadvantaged children from Toronto and its surrounding areas. Here they can experience the wilderness for a few weeks.

The new dining hall is a luminous clearing in the woods, consisting of twelve glue-lam trusses combined with lumber and light steel to make a simple wooden tent. Two-by-fours form a structural truss. The main space is thirty-six feet wide and one hundred feet long, and the roof extends beyond the exterior wall to create a large covered outdoor porch for camp activities. Raw plywood is used for the decking and the floor of the dining hall, the latter of which is painted. The dining hall glows with the life of the camp. The natural cedar siding on the exterior is detailed to weather graciously over the decades.

The dining hall is used heavily during the summer months and is closed down for the rest of the year. Wooden brises-soleil provide summer shading and fold down when not in use. A motorized greenhouse glazing system runs the length of the building along the roof ridge, bringing light into the building and providing flow-through ventilation.

The camp building has been transformed from a dark interior-focused space to one with direct physical and visual connections to the landscape, thus dissolving the zone between the building and its surroundings. As the central gathering space, the new dining hall is a major participant in enhancing the experience for its campers and shaping their memories of summer camp.

Moorelands Camp Dining Hall

1 Shaded porch and exterior walkway

2 View of the camp from the lake

3 Porch, detail

4 Camp in use

5 Dining hall

Shim-Sutcliffe Architects

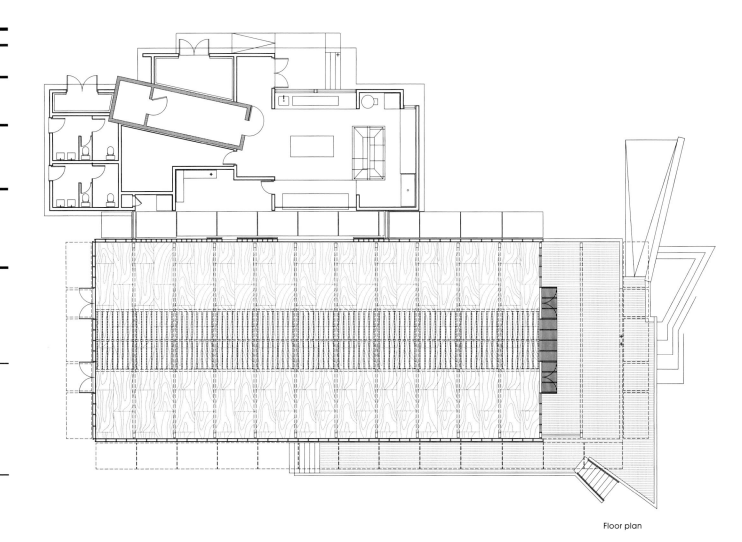

Floor plan

Moorelands Camp Dining Hall

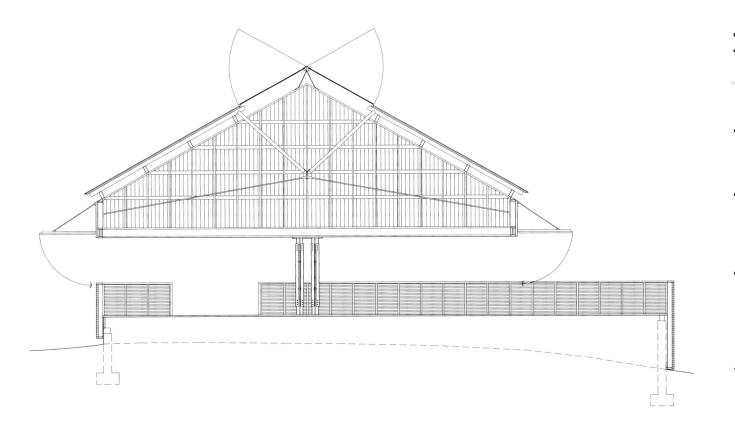

Section

latitude **61°N**
mean temperatures **JAN. 22°F**
JULY 65°F

project

WALSKY RESIDENCE

architect **Buck Walsky and Cole & Thompson Architects**
location / year Anchorage, Alaska / 2004

View from small
second-floor
deck out to lake

When artist and contractor Buck Walsky partnered with architects David and Michael Cole to build a private residence for Walsky's family on an empty lot in a well-established neighborhood in Anchorage, he knew he wanted to take advantage of the northern climate and the site's natural slope down toward a lake at the edge of the property. Therefore, he wanted to accentuate the length of the lot and pay close attention to the orientation of the sun for natural light. Opposite the lake, the lot also offers a view of the snow-covered Chugach Foothills that line the eastern edge of the city.

To play off the idea of the house as distinctly Alaskan—and because he was interested in the form—Walsky first asked Dave Cole to create a design mimicking the shape of an oil platform, while providing sufficient space for three children and a separation of private sleeping areas from the public functions of the house. Instead, the building materials themselves and the way they connect drove the design. The goal was to elevate utilitarian materials into a distinctive and sculptural structure.

Walsky wanted to incorporate surplus materials from his construction company into his home. The house rose from steel pilings and large, tempered sheets of insulated glass, a variety of glue-lams, laminated microlam wood beams, metal studs, vertical-grain fir and cedar, wood decking, stainless steel shingles, and industrial metal cabinets—all materials Walsky had collected from construction and demolition projects over many years.

The home sits on the north side of the site with a large yard, with lakeside access at the back of the house. The south side of the house is two stories to maximize openings and ways to capture sunlight; the roof slopes down toward the north and dumps the snow in an unused area of the lot. Floor and roof levels step down with the slope of the site.

Next to a window by the front door, a foot-wide slot runs the length of the house and becomes a window to the lake at the back. The slot is a unifying element that ties the street to the lake. Three simple geometric shapes—a rectangle, line, and curve—repeat and hold the design together. The exposed elements intentionally play with the idea of what "finished" implies.

East (street) facade

Walsky Residence

3

Buck Walsky and Cole & Thompson Architects

216   Walsky Residence

4 Kitchen

5 Second-floor corridor

6 Entry corridor

7 Main stair leading to second floor

Buck Walsky and Cole & Thompson Architects

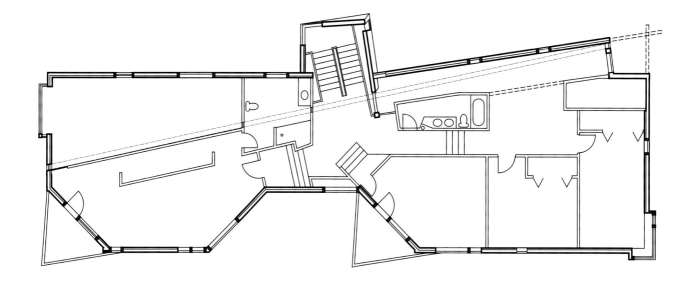

Second-floor plan

Walsky Residence

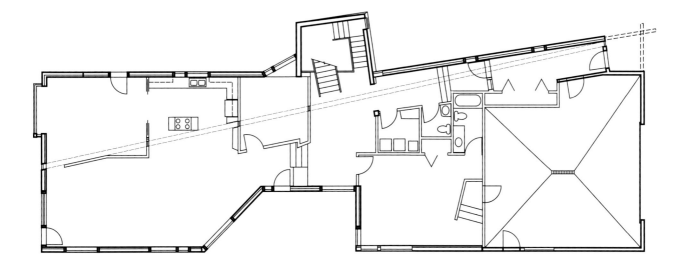

First-floor plan

FOLK ARTS CENTRE

project

architect **Lahdelma & Mahlamaki Architects**
location / year Kaustinen, Finland / 1998

Fir boarding on
the exterior

The Folk Arts Centre is an international information, training, and research center for Finnish folk culture in Kaustinen, a remote village in rural Ostrobothnia. The focus of the building is a concert hall and exhibition area. The building also houses rooms for educational and research activities, as well as the premises for the Kaustinen Folk Music Festival organization. The village celebrates its renowned folk music festival by turning its hill into an acropolis. The land east of the Gulf of Bothnia appears absolutely flat, with forests that seem to run forever in straight rows, broken only by lakes and meadows, making every hill visually important. The land in the other directions features more hills, but the city of Kaustinen is known for its flat landscape. The center's small moundlike eminence elevates it culturally and architecturally.

Putting the hall inside the hill hides its large volume, while wood cladding aligns it with surrounding structures, ensuring that a kinship in scale and material exists between the new complex and the largely timber buildings of the village. This topographical relationship to the village determined the

building's design by Lahdelma & Mahlamaki Architects. The Folk Arts Centre climbs the incline in a series of terraces connected by public stairs. These steep steps go up the hill and over the foyer, which is partly underground. On top of this hill is a dance and music pavilion, along with a sports center with a ski jump, all integrated into the center's complex.

The foyer opens up between two wings tucked underneath the outside staircase. These box forms, clad in wood lattices, hold the center's classrooms as well as the cafe and the Folk Instrument Museum, a space used for small-scale concerts and some of the exhibits. The fir boarding on the exterior is treated and made ruddy and fragrant with tar, linseed oil, and turpentine, softening the rigorous geometry. The wings emerge from the hill and guide visitors up the terraces to the entrance foyer, the spatial hub of the center.

The wood exterior contrasts with larger interior spaces of cut rock and concrete cast in wooden molds. The concert hall takes the form of an artificial cavern carved out of the hill, with raw rock walls sloping down to an ample stage. Because of the arena shape of the hall, some viewers sit on a balcony circling the stage.

Some of the smaller indoor areas counter the stark feel of rock surfaces. The Folk Instrument Museum has been exclusively constructed in wood, for example, and bleached spruce boards have also been used on the floors and walls of the building, bridging the inner space with the outer areas. Furthermore, open spaces throughout counter dimly lit areas with natural light. In the foyer, for instance, light reflects off the pale gray polished concrete floors as well as the latch boards that line most of the vertical surfaces. Lightly washed with tar, these give off a slightly smoky aroma.

Approach to the center

Folk Arts Centre

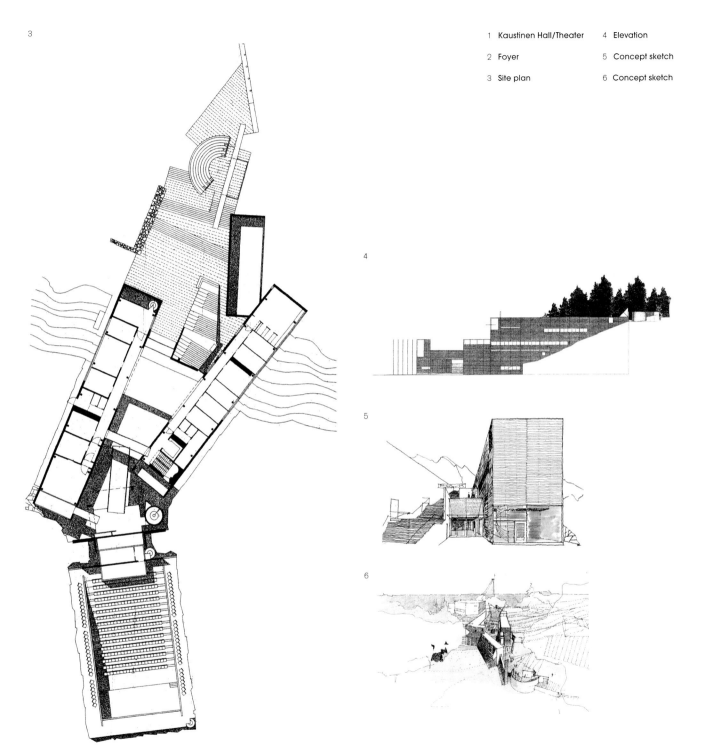

3

4

5

6

Lahdelma & Mahlamaki Architects

project # DENALI AND NORDALE PROTOTYPE SCHOOLS

---

architect **Bettisworth North**
location / year Fairbanks, Alaska / 2007

The Denali and Nordale elementary schools in Fairbanks were designed by Bettisworth North as two-story elementary prototypes for the Fairbanks North Star Borough School District. With growth projected for Alaska's school-age population, there is a demand for larger school facilities. Consequently, the state has endorsed prototype schools in order to get the best value for state dollars on school construction. Prototype schools can be built faster, more cost effectively; and, through the use of standardized building components, systems, and products, they reduce maintenance costs.

These schools replace two existing schools, each with 420 students. The entrance lobby of this prototype was designed as a continuation of the exterior pathway leading to the school, with a similar look as the street running between the educational wing and public/activity wing. The lobby serves an essential function for these schools as a beacon of light and warmth in the winter, a prominent entry and security point for school visitors, and a gathering place for students and community members.

A vertical space topped with a south-facing clerestory captures precious southern sunlight and directs it toward the north end of the building. Primary colors are used as highlights to reference the elementary school–age population and provide a contrast to the often white and gray winter days. Exposed beams in the lobby offer visible structure and the introduction of natural materials.

1 View of school from street

2 Entrance lobby

3 Second-floor plan

4 First-floor plan

Denali and Nordale Prototype Schools

3

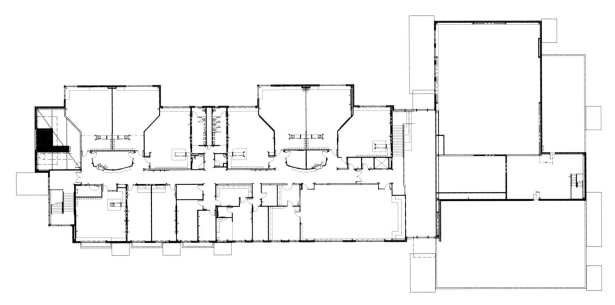

4

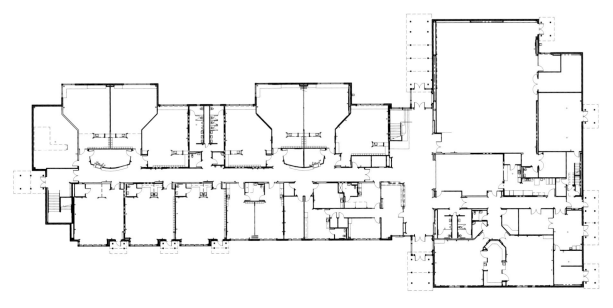

AURLAND LOOKOUT

project

architect **Saunders and Wilhelmsen**
location / year Aurland, Norway / 2008

View of the lookout
from a distance

High above the small Norwegian town of Aurland, a huge structure shaped like a ski jump juts out of the mountainside. From such a vantage point among pine trees, the Aurland Lookout affords visitors breathtaking views. Located off a snow road—a pathway created with hard-packed snow—winding through the mountains and commissioned by the Norwegian Highway Department as part of a national program on tourist routes showcasing Norway's countryside, the lookout is a piece of architecture whose beauty lies in its simplicity.

The design by Todd Saunders and Tommie Wilhelmsen involves a steel frame clad in local timber. The wood walkway springs out into the void and curves slightly back onto itself before plunging into the mountainside. The apparently seamless curve was made possible by compressed "bent" wood produced in the Netherlands. Right at the edge, before the overlook curves down, the only thing that separates the viewer from the clear blue waters of the fjord below is a glass barrier. Even the handrails continue along the vertical drop of steel and wood. The architects conceived the lookout with nature in mind: the tall pine trees

around the structure were left untouched, giving visitors a sensation of walking out into the air through the treetops.

In this way, the Aurland Lookout complements rather than competes with the magnificent scenery around it, calling attention to the snow-laden slopes and brilliant blue waters that Saunders describes as "almost mind-numbingly beautiful."

The overlook juts visitors out over a fjord.

Aurland Lookout

1 The lookout offers a variety of viewpoints from which to experience the landscape.

2 A glass barrier is the only separation between the view and the fjord below.

3 View from underneath the lookout's walkway

4 The curve of the lookout from below

Saunders and Wilhelmsen

ACKNOWLEDGMENTS

This project has been made possible by the generous support of the Anchorage Museum Building Committee, the Alaska Design Forum, and the International Gallery of Contemporary Art in Anchorage. Thank you to the architects, firms, and photographers who have contributed their creative, impressive work to be featured in this publication.

Thanks to Don Mohr for the many late-night hours spent editing photographs and line drawings, and to Dawnell Smith for her work in writing and thinking about the North. Thanks, also, to Brian Carter, Juhani Pallasmaa, Ed Crittenden, and Lisa Rochon for your expertise and wisdom.

Thanks to Mike, Annika, and Jack, who make living in the North the best way to live. This book is dedicated to northerners who brave climate and stereotypes to live life to its extremes.

PROJECT CREDITS

The New Wing of the Anchorage Museum at Rasmuson Center

Client / Anchorage Museum
Design Architect / David Chipperfield Architects
Architect of Record / Kumin Associates Incorporated
Landscape Architect / Charles Anderson Landscape Architecture
Consulting Landscape / Earthscape
Structural Engineering / BBFM Engineers, Inc.
Associate Structural Engineering / Magnusson Klemencic Associates, Inc.
MEP & IT Engineer of Record / Affiliated Engineers NW, Inc.
MEP Engineer of Record / RSA Engineering, Inc.
Civil Engineering / Tryck Nyman Hayes, Inc.
Geotechnical Engineering / DOWL HKM Engineers
Facade Consultant / W.J. Higgins & Associates, Inc.
General Contractor / Alcan General, Inc.
Photography / Larry Harris for Chris Arend Photography

Karmøy Fishing Museum

Client / Karmøy Fishing Museum
Design Architect / Snøhetta
Design Team / Craig Dykers (principal), Christoph Kapeller (principal), Kjetil Thorsen (principal), Lisbeth Funk, Knut Tronstad
Landscape Architect / Snøhetta, Ragnhild, Momrak Rainer Stange
SMEP Engineering / Peter Rasmussen
Project Administration / Construction Management / Peter Rasmussen
General Contractors / Einar Tangjerd, Kåløy, Kopervik

Ordish Anderson Residence

Client / Tanya Ordish and Ken Anderson
Architect / Kobayashi + Zedda Architects
Design Team / Antonio Zedda, Ryan McLennan
Structural Engineering / Niels Jacobsen
Mechanical Engineering / North Fraser Mechanical, Ltd.
Electrical Engineering / Action Electric, Ltd.
General Contractor / Trimate Construction, Ltd.
Photography / Kobayashi + Zedda Architects

Monastery for Cistercian Nuns

Client / Cistercian Nuns, Tautra Convent
Architect / Jensen & Skodvin
Project Team / JanOlav Jensen (principal), Børre Skodvin, Torstein Koch, Torunn Golberg, Martin Draleke, Aslak Hanshuus, Kaja Poulsen, Siri Moseng, AnneLise Bjerkan
Landscape Architect / The nuns and local professionals
Static Consultant / Dr. Techn. Kristoffer Apeland

St. Henry's Ecumenical Art Chapel

Investor / Client: St. Henry's Chapel Association
Architect / Sanaksenaho Architects, Ltd.
Design Team / Matti Sanaksenaho, Pirjo Sanaksenaho
Project Team / Sari Lehtonen, Enrico Garbin, Teemu Kurkela, Juha Jääskeläinen, Maria Isotupa, Jaana Hellinen, Jari Mänttäri, Kain Tapper
Glass Artist / Hannu Konola
Structural Engineering / Kalevi Narmala
HVAC Engineering / Juhani Lehtonen
Electrical Engineering / Taneli Mussaari
Constructor / Hartela

Villa in Archipelago

Client / Private
Architect / Tham & Videgård Hansson Architects
Design Team / Bolle Tham and Martin Videgård Hansson
Photography / Åke E:son Lindman

Skrudas Residence

Client / Private
Architect / Studio Granda
Structure and Services Engineering / Vidsjá
Electrical Engineering / Verfraedistofan Johanns Indridasonar
Photography / Sigurgeir Sigurjónsson

Buser/Chapoton Residence

Client / Buser/Chapoton
Architect / mayer sattler-smith
Structural Engineering / Jim Loftus
General Contractor / Happy Trails

Hotel Kirkenes

Client / Pikene på Broen, Via Travels

Architect / Sami Rintala

Construction Team / Sami Rintala, George Lovett
(architecture student, University of Sheffield, UK),
Borghild Hulsvik (architecture student, Bergen
Architect School), Anne Kathrine Vabø (architecture
student, Bergen Architect School)

Sponsors / Nicopan (windows), Jotun (paint)

Photography / Morten Torgersrud, Sami Rintala, Jan Erik
Svendsen

Petter Dass Museum

Client / KF Petter Dass Eiendom

Architect / Snøhetta

Project Team / Kjetil T. Thorsen, Tarald Lundevall, Astrid
Renata Van Veen, Maria Svaland, Jim Dodson,
Bartosz Milewski, Tom Holtmann, Ellen Heier, Andreas
Nygaard, Heidi Pettersvold, Jenny Osuldsen, Lars
Nordbye Jørstad

Photography / Åke E:son Lindman

Village Schools

Client / Yupiit School District

Architect / Koonce Pfeffer Bettis Architects

General Contractor / UIC (Tuluksak), SKW (Akiak and
Akiachak)

Consultants / DOWL Engineers, Coffman Engineers,
MC Squared, Inc., HMS RWDI, Mullins Acoustics,
Aurora Corporate Enterprises

Photography / Kevin G. Smith

Rovaniemi Airport

Client / Finnish Civil Aviation Administration

Architect / Heikkinen-Komonen Architects

Design Team / Mikko Heikkinen and Markku Komonen

Project Architect / Mikko Rossi

Construction Engineering / Insinööritoimisto Konstru

HVAC Engineering / Projectus

Electrical Engineering / Projectus

General Contractor / YIT-Rakennus

Photography / Jussi Tiainen

Longyearbyen Research Centre, Svalbard University

Client / Statsbygg/Norwegian Directorate of Public
Construction and Property

Architect / Jarmund/Vigsnæs

Design Team / Einar Jarmund, Håkon Vigsnæs,
Alessandra Kosberg, assisted by Anders Granli,
Nevzat Vize, Sissil Morseth Gromholt, Thor
Christian Pethon, Halina Noach, Harald Lode,
Stian Schjelderup

Structural Engineering / Frederiksen

Electrical Engineering / Monstad

Mechanical Engineering / Erichsen & Horgen

Landscape Architect / Grindaker

HVAC Engineering / Byggforsk Thomas Thiis

Photography / Nils Petter

BP Energy Center

Client / BP Exploration Alaska, Inc.

Architect and Interior Design / Koonce Pfeffer Bettis
Architects

General Contractor / Boslough Construction

Mechanical Engineering / Hay, Zietlow and Associates

Electrical Engineering / EIC

Civil Engineering / DOWL Engineers

Structural Engineering / PDC

Exhibit Consultants / Ear Studio

Photography / Kevin G. Smith

Dänojà Zho Cultural Centre

Client / Tr'ondek Hwech'in First Nation

Architect / Maurer Kobayashi Architects (now
Kobayashi + Zedda Architects)

Structural Engineering / Wood & Associates
Structural Engineers

Mechanical Engineering / Northern Climate Engineering

Electrical Engineering / Dorward Engineering Services

Nearpoint House

Owner/Client / Richard Navitsky and Tanya Leinicke

Architect / Workshop for Architecture and Design

Project Team / Steven Bull, Dan Rusler, Marty McElveen

Consultants / Harriott Engineers

Hof Residence

Clients / Lilja Pálmadóttir & Baltasar Kormákur Baltasarsson
Architect / Studio Granda
Structural and Environmental Engineering / Vídsja
Electrical Services / VJÍ
General Contractor / Trésmidjan Borg

Old Crow Visitor's Center

Client / Vuntut Gwitchin First Nation
Architect / Kobayashi + Zedda Architects
Project Manager / Building Industry Consultants
Structural Engineering / NA Jacobsen Civil Engineer
Mechanical Engineering / Lessoway Moir Partners
Electrical Engineering / Dorward Engineering
General Contractor / Weitzel's Construction

Phelps/Burke Residence

Client / Private
Architect / mayer sattler-smith
Structural Engineering / Jim Loftus
Construction / Wintersun Construction
Photography / Kevin G. Smith

Maassen/Gouwens Residence

Client / Peter Maassen and Kay Gouwens
Architect / Black + White Studio Architects
General Contractor / Dawson Development
Photography / Kevin G. Smith

Birch Hill Ski Building

Client / Fairbanks North Star Borough
Architect / Bettisworth North
General Contractor / Richard Stanton Construction
Mechanical Engineering / Hay Zietlow and Associates, LLC
Electrical and Structural Engineering / PDC, Inc.
Civil, Water Engineering / Lifewater Engineering
Civil, Soils Engineering / R & M Consultants, Inc.
Environmental Engineering / Harding ESE
Cost Estimating / HMS, Inc.
Photography / Kevin G. Smith

Laugalækjarskóli Secondary School Addition

Client / City of Reykjavík
Architect / Studio Granda
Structural Engineering / VSÓ
Electrical Engineering / VJÍ
Contractor / Trésmiðjan Borg
Service Engineering / VGK
Photography / Studio Granda

Tantalus School

Client / Yukon Public Schools (Tantalus School)
Architect / Kobayashi + Zedda Architects
Structural Engineering / Fast + Epp Partners with NA Jacobsen Civil Engineering
Mechanical Engineering / Lessoway Moir & Associates
Electrical Engineering / Dorward Engineering Services
Seismic Engineering / M. Wang & Associates
General Contractor / Dowland Contracting
Mechanical Engineering / Duncans
Electrical Engineering / Arcrite Northern
Painting / Fireweed Painting

Mountain Cabin

Client / Private
Architect / div.A Architects
General Contractor / Bøygard Bygg
Photography / Michael Perlmutter

Mountain Lodge

Client / Stavanger Turistforening (Stavanger Trekking Association)
Architect / Helen & Hard

Summerhouse

Client / Saunders and Wilhelmsen
Architect / Saunders and Wilhelmsen
Carpenter / Mats Odin Rustøy (architecture student)

Davis Residence

Client / Tom and Laura Davis
Architect / Black + White Studio Architects
General Contractor / Tom and Laura Davis, Tom Davis Sr.
Photography / Kevin G. Smith

Mitton Residence

Client / Andrew and Michelle Mitton
Architect / Black + White Studio Architects
General Contractor / Summitview Construction
Photography / Kevin G. Smith

Moorelands Camp Dining Hall

Client / Downtown Churchworkers Association
Architect / Shim-Sutcliffe Architects
Design Team / Brigitte Shim (principal), Howard
Sutcliffe (principal), Jason Emery Groen
Presentation Drawings / Min Wang
Structural Engineering / Dave Bowick, Blackwell Engineering
Constructor / Gord McLean and crew
Photography / Michael Awad, James Dow

Walsky Residence

Client / Buck and Agnes Walsky
Architect / Buck Walsky and Cole & Thompson Architects
Design Team / M. David Cole, Michael Cole, Buck Walsky
Structural Engineering / Nelson Franklin
General Contractor and Construction / Buck Walsky

Folks Arts Centre

Architect / Lahdelma & Mahlamaki Architects
Architects / Rainer Mahlamäki, Juha Mäki-Jyllilä
Interior Design / Gullstén Inkinen

Denali and Nordale Prototype Schools

Client / Fairbanks North Star Borough School District, Department of Public Works
Architect / Bettisworth North
General Contractor / Jim Christianson of
Collins Construction
Mechanical, Electrical Engineering / DEJONG, Inc.
Civil, Survey Engineering / Design Alaska, Inc.
Structural Engineering / BBFM Engineers, Inc.
Geotechnical Engineering / Shannon & Wilson, Inc.
Landscape Architecture / Earthscape
Photography / Kevin G. Smith Photography

Aurland Lookout

Client / Norwegian Highways Department
Architects / Saunders and Wilhelmsen
Technical Advisors / Node
General Contractor / Veidekke
Road Engineering / Asplan Viak
Photography / Todd Saunders

CONTRIBUTER BIOGRAPHIES

JULIE DECKER is a director of the International Gallery of Contemporary Art in Anchorage and a frequent guest art curator at the Anchorage Museum, currently working on exhibitions and publications on contemporary art for children, contemporary art of the circumpolar North, and northern architecture. She is also an instructor of art history at the University of Alaska. Decker has written numerous articles and publications on the art and architecture of Alaska, including *John Hoover: Art & Life* (2002), *Icebreakers: Alaska's Most Innovative Artists* (1999), *Found & Assembled in Alaska* (2000), and *Quonset: Metal Living for a Modern Age* (Princeton Architectural Press, 2005). She lives in Anchorage with her husband, her children Annika and Jack, and her two dogs.

BRIAN CARTER is an architect practicing in the United Kingdom. He received his professional diploma in architecture from the Nottingham School of Architecture in England and a master's degree in architecture from the University of Toronto. Carter is the author of a number of books, including *Johnson Wax Administration Building and Research Tower (Architecture in Detail)* (1998) and *Patkau Architects: Selected Projects 1983–1993* (1994); a contributor to *Ghost: Building an Architectural Vision* (Princeton Architectural Press, 2008); and a contributor to numerous architectural journals. His scholarly work focuses on design research through practice and the consideration of modernism in contemporary architecture.

EDWIN B. CRITTENDEN was an active architect and community planner in private practice for most of his career. He graduated from Pomona College (1938), received his architecture degree from Yale University (1942), and did graduate studies at the Massachusetts Institute of Technology (1948–49). Crittenden moved to Alaska in 1943 and served in various technical positions. He was appointed to the Alaska State Technical Review Board for the Historic Preservation Act (later the Historic Sites Advisory Board) in 1970, on which he served until 1977. He was owner/principal of an Anchorage-based architectural firm, which underwent numerous name changes but was best known as CCC/HOK (Crittenden-Cassetta-Cannon/Hellmuth-Obata-Kassabaum). He has written extensively on cold-climate construction.

JUHANI PALLASMAA practices architecture and product design, as well as exhibition and graphic design, through Juhani Pallasmaa Architects in Helsinki. He lectures and writes extensively on the philosophy of architecture, architectural criticism, the phenomenology of art, and the relationships between architecture and cinema. Pallasmaa received his diploma in architecture from the Helsinki University of Technology (1966). He was professor of architecture at Helsinki University of Technology (1991–97) and dean of the Faculty of Architecture (1993–96), and has taught in various universities in Europe, North and South America, and Africa. He has published numerous books and exhibition catalogues, including The *Eyes of the Skin: Architecture and the Senses* (2005).

LISA ROCHON is the architecture critic for the Toronto *Globe and Mail* and the two-time winner of the National Newspaper Awards for Arts and Entertainment (2005, 2006). She is the author of *UP NORTH: Where Canada's Architecture Meets the Land* (2004). From 1998 to 2004, Rochon was an adjunct professor at the University of Toronto's Faculty of Architecture, Landscape, and Design. Rochon speaks regularly across Canada about architecture. She holds an MA in Urban Design Studies from the University of Toronto. Her bachelor's degree in journalism and in French was completed at Carleton University, Ottawa.

IMAGE CREDITS

90°N
80°N
70°N

60°N

50°N

40°N

30°N

20°N

10°N

0°